16$\frac{95}{6}$

SPEAKING FOR SUCCESS

The Canadian Guide

SPEAKING FOR SUCCESS
The Canadian Guide

ANTHONY LIEB
Georgian College

HARCOURT
BRACE
CANADA

Harcourt Brace & Company, Canada

Toronto Montreal Fort Worth New York Orlando
Philadelphia San Diego London Sydney Tokyo

Canadian Cataloguing in Publication Data

Lieb, Anthony
    Speaking for Success : the
    Canadian guide

ISBN 0-7747-3211-3

1. Public Speaking. 2. Oratory. I. Title.

PN4121.L43 1993   808.5'1   C92-095185-6

Editorial Director: *Heather McWhinney*
Acquisitions Editor: *Michael J. Young*
Developmental Editor: *Nancy S. Ennis*
Editorial Manager: *Marcel Chiera*
Production Manager: *Sue-Ann Becker*
Interior Design: *Lorne Finnerty*
Illustrator: *William Kimber*
Technical Art: *Debbie Fleming*
Cover Design: *Dave Peters*
Cover Photography: *Susan Dobson*
Printing and Binding: *Best Gagné Book Manufacturers*

This book was printed in Canada on acid-free paper.
4 5 6 7   98 99 00 01

Other Titles Available in the *Harbrace Guides to Student Success* Series

Fit to Print: The Canadian Student's Guide to Essay Writing, 2/e by Joanne Buckley

Learning for Success: Skills and Strategies for Canadian Students by Joan Fleet, Fiona Goodchild, and Richard Zajchowski

Career Success: The Canadian Guide by Shannon Whelan

"I couldn't have made a better choice than to buy *Fit to Print*. It was and is a life saver! Since that day I haven't received a mark below 80% on my essays."

Joanne R.
Harbord Collegiate Institute

"*Fit to Print* takes a clear, concise, no-nonsense approach to the problems of essay writing. Students (especially first-year students) will be able to understand this compact text and will not have to wade through it--as is the case with so many discursive composition books."

William Benzie
University of Victoria

"For its emphasis on well-written prose and its easy-to-follow, practical approach, *Fit to Print* is an invaluable aid for student writers in any discipline. Few books offer so much practical information to change student writing from a struggle to a success."

Jim MacDonald & Karen Jakob
Humber College

"*Learning for Success* is the book I used most during my first three weeks back at school. Returning to school after twelve years, I found this to be the most helpful of all my textbooks in real, practical terms. I would highly recommend this book for anyone just entering college or returning to school after having been away from the classroom for some time."

David Beattie
Peterborough

"For students who want to improve their study skills *Learning for Success* is an excellent resource. It explains the theory of study skills in understandable language, gives examples and asks for student response."

Carol Potter
Dawson College

"We offer a series of seminars, called 'Learning for Success' after this book. It is a lucid, concise, orderly and comprehensive, and serves a valuable purpose."

David Nimmo
University of Toronto

"*Learning for Success* is an excellent, practical guide for students in college and university, as well as senior high school level. It is a great resource for beginning counsellors, as it provides valuable information on various topics related to student success."

Irmo Marini
Counselling Coordinator
Lakehead University

"*Career Success*" is a practical, positive, and useful guide for anyone who is seeking a fulfilling career. High school students, college students, and adults looking for a career change--all will benefit from the practical advice and encouragement that the author gives."

Lindsay Holmes
Student
University of Calgary

This text is dedicated to

my parents

CONTENTS

CHAPTER 8
The Formal Meeting

PREFACE

People in school or business engage in two distinct types of speaking--conversational and presentational. As the name implies, conversational speaking involves people engaging in informal, relaxed dialogue. Opinions are shared, questions are asked and answered, information is exchanged.

Many good conversational speakers experience discomfort and difficulty whenever they find themselves behind a podium. This presentational environment often inhibits the fluid, relaxed style most speakers are capable of and use daily. When finding themselves on stage, speakers realize that many variables not a part of conventional conversation play a role in the success of their formal presentations.

Speaking for Success was written with two assumptions: that if you can carry on relaxed conversations, you have the ability to be an effective presentational speaker; and that the understanding and application of basic presentation planning strategies and techniques will give you a relaxed and effective delivery.

As part of the "Student Success Series," *Speaking for Success* provides you with topical information in a critical academic area. Its companion texts--*Learning for Success, Fit to Print*, and *Career Success*--already offer excellent instruction in specific communication areas.

The Market

This book was designed with two distinct audiences in mind. As a textbook, it addresses the needs of students and instructors of college and university oral communications courses. Its structure and length make it ideal for one-semester speaking courses and as a companion text in lengthier communications programs.

Today, many businesses and service organizations interact more frequently with the public. As a reference text, this book serves as a concise guide to in-house and external oral communication. Professionals with little or no speech training or speaking experience should benefit from this straightforward approach to public speaking.

Goals of the Text

Speaking for Success is a guide to the various types of speeches students and professionals are most likely to present. The text is designed to meet the demands of current college and university speech courses and the business world. Because most college and university public speaking courses are one-semester practical courses, this book provides the essential theoretical elements of public speaking in an encapsulated form. It is, more than anything, a reference book offering guidance on how to prepare and deliver the more popular varieties of oral presentation. In addition to discussing the components of individual and group presentations, the book provides chapters on two common areas of concern--speech anxiety and visual aids.

Features of the Text

Central to the design of the text is the belief that people who want to become better speakers should speak before an audience at every opportunity. Consequently, the book covers the essential features of public speaking without excessive commentary and examples. Each chapter is prefaced by an introduction that provides the pivotal background information necessary to get the most out of the text.

Terms that may be unfamiliar or that have a specific oral communication connotation appear in bold face. These boldfaced words and phrases reappear at the end of the book in a glossary.

The content of each chapter is clearly divided by headings and subheadings to help clarify the process of presentation construction and delivery. Most chapters also provide a planning guide so you can apply the points covered in the planning and development of your own speech. Since this book's binding allows it to open flat at any page, these planning guides can also serve as speech outlines for use at the podium.

Because speech evaluation is an important part of any practical public speaking course, both individual and group adjudication forms are provided. They are designed to be photocopied and used by student and instructor alike as part of the evaluation process.

Structure of the Text

The sequence of the chapters is designed to facilitate the development of effective oral skills. *Speaking for Success* contains three general categories of speech-related material: individual presentations, group presentations, and peripheral information. The book begins with the chapter Coping with Speech Anxiety, which addresses the concerns of all speakers, new and experienced. It explores the causes of speech stress and offers suggestions for overcoming the negative effects of this common affliction.

The second chapter, Nonverbal Communication, presents the various ways speakers transmit messages with their bodies and the effects these messages have on the audience. By understanding how posture, gesture, and facial expression contribute to the effectiveness of oral communication, you can enhance the clarity of your messages and reduce the chance of misinterpretation.

Chapter 3 describes the types of visual aids currently available and how to apply them when making a speech or conducting a meeting. The figures in this chapter illustrate the diversity of visual aids that may be employed.

Chapter 4, Adjudication: Evaluating the Presentation, discusses the factors that determine the success of a speech. This chapter explains the terminology used on adjudication forms and how speakers should be evaluated. Individual and group adjudication forms are included for use by markers.

Chapters 5 and 6, The Informative Speech and The Persuasive Speech, describe the varieties of individual presentation and their construction. Sample speech outlines are provided for you at the conclusion of each chapter.

The final two chapters explore group presentations. Chapter 7, The Small Group Presentation, describes strategies employed in symposia, debates, and panel discussions. In addition to considering the roles and responsibilities of group members, the chapter shows you the differences between these presentations by providing specific examples.

Chapter 8, The Formal Meeting, begins with a discussion of the characteristics and limitations of a meeting. It outlines the duties of the meeting officers and establishes the importance of documentation in the formal meeting process. The balance of the chapter discusses the rules governing formal meeting procedure.

ACKNOWLEDGEMENTS

No book is solely the product of its author and, like other texts, *Speaking for Success: The Canadian Guide* owes much to many individuals. I received valuable assistance from the editorial staff of HBJ-Holt Canada. My editors--Heather McWhinney, Nancy Ennis, and especially Michael Young--were extremely patient and supportive. I thank them all for their guidance and encouragement. The technical advice and expertise provided by Dr. Lorne Finnerty and Dr. Brent Kloczko contributed immeasurably to the chapter dealing with speech anxiety and to the ultimate appearance of the book.

Much of the content and approach of the book is the direct result of the constructive criticism provided by the following reviewers:

Susan Braley, Betty Lucas, Debra Meredith, Richard Pentney, Jim Streeter, and John Swiderski.

Dr. Bill Elwood and the students of Advanced Public Speaking at the University of South Florida (USF) graciously allowed me to sit in on a number of their classes. Two USF students, Tanya Lance and Jennifer Malin, provided outlines for inclusion in this text. I am also indebted to my students and colleagues at Georgian College. Their commitment to learning and teaching excellence has been inspirational.

Anthony Lieb
Sarasota, Florida
June 1992

Publisher's Note to Instructors and Students

This textbook is a key component of your course. If you are the instructor of this course, you undoubtedly considered a number of texts carefully before choosing this as the one that would work best for your students and you. The author and publishers spent considerable time and money to ensure its high quality, and we appreciate your recognition of this effort and accomplishment. Please note the copyright statement.

If you are a student, we are confident that this text will help you to meet the objectives of your course. It will also become a valuable addition to your personal library.

Since we want to hear what you think about this book, please be sure to send us the stamped reply card at the end of the text. Your input will help us to continue to publish high-quality books for your courses.

CHAPTER 1

Coping With Speech Anxiety

- Types of Stress
- Responses to Speech Stress
- Controlling Speech Anxiety

What's the first feeling you get when you think about giving a speech to a large number of people? Is it nervousness, a tightening of the throat, a feeling of butterflies in the stomach? If it is, you're not alone. Most of us have a dread of speech making because we associate it with feelings of stress. Even professional actors, athletes, and singers, despite their experience, still become anxious--often quite seriously--before a public performance. Why is it that people can perform naturally and effectively before one or a few viewers but become nervous in front of a larger audience? Researchers still aren't sure. But the thought of speaking before an assembly affects over 90 percent of speakers, both professional and amateur, with the same result--nervousness.

This first chapter will explore the nature and causes of speech anxiety, also known as speech stress, stage fright, or performance anxiety. It will look at how speech anxiety is manifested in most people and how you can learn to control it.

Types of Stress

Being nervous is a natural component of public speaking. In fact, if you don't show any anxiety while you deliver a speech, your audience might think you don't care about what you're saying or that you are uninspired. Nervousness seems to indicate that you care enough about the task to do well.

The stress created before and during public speaking becomes a problem only when it gets out of your control. There is an ideal balance between tension and comfort that you should strive for when you are speaking in public.

It is important to remember that people vary in their responses to speech stress. Each person's inherent stress level is unique. When it is coupled with other factors, such as situational stress and hereditary stress, a very personal stress profile emerges. As a result, the success rates of stress management techniques vary among individuals.

Let's take a closer look at the types of stress that can work together to create performance anxiety. Like all speakers, you will experience a combination of several different **stressors**.

Baseline Stress

The factor most influential on your performance under pressure is **baseline stress**. Baseline stress is your average stress level at any given time. Each of us is born with a certain baseline stress, but with practice, we can learn to modify it.

Critical Stress

Part of the baseline stress equation, **critical stress** is the fixed or constant stress point at which apprehension causes your performance to suffer. It is at this threshold that physiological or psychological manifestations make you aware of pressure. If you don't control these stress symptoms, your audience will also become aware of your discomfort.

If you can reduce your baseline stress, you can increase the buffer zone between it and your critical threshold. This will help you to endure more stress before it becomes apparent to you and the audience. Baseline stress has been successfully lowered through the use of biofeedback, changes in diet and sleep patterns, and preparation techniques.

Trait Anxiety and State Anxiety

Two other factors may also play important roles in your response to stress. **Trait anxiety** is believed to be a trait genetically acquired by every individual to some degree. It seems closely linked to baseline stress. People who demonstrate high trait anxiety experience stress as a constant, palpable element in their day-to-day lives--whether or not they have a stressful task to perform. With the introduction of a major stressor, such as public speaking, these individuals become further agitated, and their performance may suffer as a result.

Another factor that may affect your response to stress is **state anxiety**. Most people who exhibit stress symptoms are subject to this progressive discomfort. State anxiety first arises when a task that is negatively perceived is assigned. After this initial anxiety, individuals usually return to their previous baseline stress level. But as the deadline for the task approaches, the anxiety attacks tend to increase in frequency and magnitude. Immediately before performing the task, most people experience their strongest wave of state anxiety--but they usually overcome their nervousness and perform well once they get started.

The evidence seems to indicate that most people are subject to a combination of trait and state anxieties. Those experiencing a high level of trait anxiety are most seriously influenced by stress, but all people can respond more positively to pressure by concentrating on their baseline stress levels.

One Solution?

Unfortunately, there is no single antidote to stress. The degree to which a speaker is affected by each stressor varies from person to person, and you must learn to understand yourself and the factors that most influence your performance before you can effectively manage your individual responses to speech anxiety.

Speech Anxiety Factors

Three primary factors will influence your performance before an audience. They are the audience, the subject of your speech, and you, the speaker. Every speaker is influenced by these factors to varying degrees.

The Audience

Probably your greatest source of concern as a speaker is the audience. In our culture, we tend to link good articulation skills with intelligence, so naturally we all want to do well when speaking--whether to a few people or to a crowd. We feel more relaxed when we're speaking to one or a few listeners because the stakes are lower: if we do poorly, only a few listeners will witness our failure. As a result, we rarely experience severe speech anxiety and usually perform effectively. But with experience comes a shift in attitude. Rather than thinking of a large group as a large number of potential witnesses to failure, you'll begin to think more positively. The larger the numbers, the more people can appreciate your success.

The professional and educational status of your audience will also influence your level of comfort on stage. You may feel less intimidated addressing audiences below your professional or academic level, and yet you'll probably feel a higher sense of achievement if you perform well before an expert audience. Teachers are a prime example of this phenomenon. Because they are more knowledgeable than the people they are instructing, they feel comfortable and confident speaking in front of their students. Those same teachers are invariably more anxious addressing an expert audience, such as other teachers or administrators, and yet will experience a higher degree of satisfaction if they do well in front of this kind of crowd.

Your familiarity with the people in the audience can also affect your performance. Most speakers feel much more relaxed addressing a group of friends than a group of strangers. Friends are more forgiving and less judgmental, while strangers represent the unknown. You can't accurately predict their reactions.

Even seating arrangements can change the way you relate comfortably to a gathering. A large space, such as a gymnasium, can be intimidating. All the seats face the stage in a seemingly confrontational manner, and you're obviously outnumbered. Try to have the seats placed in a smaller space or in a different configuration, such as a semicircle around you. Such an arrangement will feel far less threatening and will give a much greater sense of intimacy. Of course, you won't always have the option of rearranging the seats, but you *can* often move closer to your audience. This adjustment in proximity can increase your rapport with the assembly.

A last word on audiences: although many speakers expect the worst of an audience and deliver their speeches with that expectation, the vast majority of audiences are friendly and empathetic. They want the speaker to do well. After all, that's why they've invested their time and effort to attend.

The Subject

The better you know your subject matter, the more at ease you'll be when presenting it. You'll appear more relaxed because you won't need to rely on your prepared notes as much. Familiarity requires practice. Constant rehearsal will help your presentation sound considered and relaxed.

The level of difficulty of your subject matter can also influence your delivery. First of all, it's important that *you* fully understand your material. Your task is then to pass on this understanding to your audience. You should aim to present your material at an interesting and comprehensible level. Present it at too high a level and your audience won't understand it. But present it at too low a level and your audience won't be challenged to think. In either case, the assembly will lose interest and tune out. To be successful, try to think ahead about the makeup of your audience. Consider its ability to comprehend your material as you prepare it.

And the topic itself? Perhaps you want to focus your speech on a contentious issue. Bear in mind that a controversial subject is more likely to create stress in a speaker than a "safe" one. But if you can handle it, give it a try. Controversial topics usually elicit a great listener response. If you think you'd find a really important topic too intimidating, or doubt that you could do justice to it, choose something a little more manageable. But at all costs, avoid choosing a subject you feel is unimportant. Its chance for success is minimal. You'll perform well if you feel your topic is worthwhile, but if it isn't, you'll probably have difficulty motivating yourself to properly prepare and deliver your speech. And the audience will likely find it a waste of time.

You, The Speaker

Think for a moment of how you felt before your last visit to the dentist's office. Anxious, perhaps? Put together a prior bad experience and the unknown awaiting you in the dentist's chair and that's enough to create anxiety. In fact, it is that period of waiting and anticipation that's the most stressful part of any negative task. Once it is begun, most people concentrate on the matter at hand, become task-oriented, and lose their prior anxiety.

It's the same with public speaking. Maybe you've had one or more negative public speaking experiences. If you have, you may feel like giving up and never appearing before an audience again. It can be very embarrassing to feel you've failed in front of a crowd. Yet the audience probably didn't think you were as terrible as you yourself imagined. Most of the symptoms of stress you felt on stage were imperceptible to the audience. Usually, you are your own harshest critic.

But doing poorly is, in fact, an important component of the learning process. If you've had some bad experiences, don't worry--and don't give up. Like most activities, public speaking requires a collection of skills that you can improve with practice.

Your attitude to the audience can also make a big difference to your performance on stage. If you think of the audience as hostile, you'll speak and act defensively. Everyone has witnessed the performance of a reluctant speaker-- the cowering posture, the nervous twitches, the rising **intonation**. This type of reaction inhibits the speaker from making a successful speech and distresses the audience. Once you have learned through experience that audiences are generally expectant and friendly, you'll be able to relax and perform to your potential.

If you think you're not going to do well, you probably won't.   Adopt a positive attitude about your task and you demonstrate high self-esteem--a quality that can help you in this, and any other, stressful situation.

Speech Anxiety Symptoms

Now you've taken a look at the factors that can affect your own particular brand of speech anxiety. But before you can begin to manage the stress you feel about public speaking, it's important to understand how stress is actually caused and what kinds of symptoms it can produce.

Pretend you are preparing for a speaking engagement. You begin to imagine worst-case scenarios and become increasingly nervous as the deadline for your speech draws near. By the time the big day arrives, you feel terrified. Inevitably, your psychological fears cause a physiological response. You stutter and blush on the podium, and these physiological symptoms further unnerve you. The experience is mortifying. You are shocked by your inability to control your emotions and your body, and you are convinced that you are the one person in the world who is totally incapable of giving a speech.

But wait. You shouldn't be surprised that stress has a powerful effect on you. Each person's emotional and physical reactions to stress will be different--but everyone is affected by it. The physiological symptoms aggravate the psychological ones; the psychological symptoms amplify the physical ones. And it's your confidence that suffers.

Let's trace the process of exactly how speech anxiety affects your body so that we can learn how to break this chain of responses.

"Fight or Flight"

The first thing that creates stress in a public speaker is the assignment of the task. Seconds after you learn that you must address an audience, your body has already begun to react. Chemicals, most notably **adrenalin**, or **epinephrine**, are released into your bloodstream. These powerful hormones prepare your body to meet a threat or challenge. The adrenalin, when it reaches your heart, speeds up your heart rate. You'll feel this accelerated heart rate in your chest and "hear" it in your ears. It will quickly raise your blood pressure, resulting in the first outward evidence of stress.

This is the **sympathetic nervous system**'s response to a stimulus. Although you cannot prevent this process, you *can* choose how you will cope with the symptoms. After quickly assessing the challenge, you may instinctively elect one of two options: **fight** or **flight**.

If you find the threat overpowering, you may choose to flee from the danger. The result on the podium? You will likely speak rapidly in an attempt to flee the stage as quickly as possible. It's not uncommon for speakers who average a delivery rate of 160 words per minute to speak well in excess of 200 words per minute when in flight.

If, on the other hand, you decide the threat is manageable and you opt to fight, again your speech will be affected. Speakers who choose to fight struggle with each and every word on stage, refusing to give in to their fears until the speech has been completed. They tend to speak markedly slower than usual, often as slowly as 100 words per minute.

Is there another option? Yes, and it's the best one. Ideally, you won't choose to fight or flee. If you accept the task with an attitude that is neither escapist nor confrontational, your style will be relaxed and you will pace your delivery well.

Physiological Responses

The body responds to stress in many ways. Here are some responses that may be anticipated:

Blushing and Perspiration

When chemicals surge through your body and your blood pressure goes up, more blood is being delivered to all parts of your body, including the blood vessels, or **capillaries**, near the skin's surface. When these small vessels become gorged with blood, they increase the colour and temperature of the skin surface: in other words, you blush. Blushing is most obvious around your face and neck, where there are lots of capillaries. Because skin temperature goes up, you'll usually find that you perspire on your face and neck, the body's way of cooling the skin surface.

Fluid-related Symptoms and Shivering

Some people experience fluid-related symptoms when under stress, such as a dryness in the mouth or an increased need to urinate. Uncontrollable shivering is another symptom experienced by individuals under stress. A common response to immediate pressure, shivering is most often caused by the sudden cooling of the skin surface. It can also be accompanied by "goose bumps."

Hyperventilation

Hyperventilation is another direct response to the "fight or flight" syndrome. When your body is faced by a threat, it requires more oxygen to prepare for action. When you breathe more quickly and more deeply, you are delivering extra oxygen to your lungs and then, via the bloodstream, to your muscles and organs. If you hyperventilate for too long, you can begin to feel dizzy or giddy--a feeling that can add to existing anxiety.

Stuttering and Stammering

The most apparent manifestations of stress to an audience are **stuttering** and **stammering**. Stuttering is the jerky, usually rapid repetition of the same sound. Stammering is the more obvious physical struggle to speak, resulting in repetitions and hesitations. Both phenomena are caused when your breathing patterns are disrupted. If you don't have enough air in your lungs, you won't be able to speak without effort. This can make your speech more difficult to understand, and it can undermine your self-assurance.

"Butterflies" and Fidgeting

And then there are the familiar "butterflies in the stomach" or "heartburn." These symptoms are caused by the increased secretion of acid in your stomach, an autonomic or involuntary response. In extreme instances, this high acid concentration can contribute to nausea. Fortunately, the acid is usually quickly neutralized when the waiting period is over and you begin your speech.

Even if you rarely display restlessness, you may find yourself pacing or fidgeting before performing a stressful task. If you have a tendency toward **hyperactivity** or trait anxiety, you are especially susceptible to the added strain of a stressful task.

Psychological Responses

Stress doesn't just affect your body--it also affects your mind. If you have a low baseline stress, you will demonstrate few emotional responses to anxiety. If you have a high baseline stress, you'll show more emotional responses. Here are some of the psychological responses to look for:

Disorganization

The most common psychological symptom of stress is disorganization. Even if you are well-prepared to meet the challenges posed by a stressor, you can experience a temporary disorganization caused by second-guessing or last-minute revisions. In its severest form, disorganization can lead to mental confusion. You might feel unable to concentrate or maintain a logical order of elements.

Memory Loss

Do you worry about forgetting every word of your speech as soon as you step onto the podium? When you're under pressure, you can experience a memory loss, forgetting information that is "overlearned" or memorized. This "blanking out" usually only lasts a few seconds--but they can be an anxiety-laden few seconds! In most instances, a visual prompt such as a word or picture restores memory quickly and completely.

Disorientation

Disorientation--the loss of a sense of place, direction, or time--is the rarest and most severe reaction to a stressful situation. In some cases disorientation is accompanied by **vertigo** or severe dizziness. Those demonstrating disorientation and vertigo are incapable of performing their duties until the stressor is removed.

Controlling Speech Anxiety

There's no doubt about it: public speaking is stressful. Speech anxiety or stage fright is an inevitable part of public speaking. But the anticipation of public speaking and the performance itself should be exciting, challenging experiences, not painful ones. You can't let one or two poor public speaking performances put you off ever speaking in public again. You've got to get over that embarrassment, and spend time learning the skills of public speaking--skills that are simply remedies to stress.

Speech anxiety doesn't have to control you. Now that you know something about what it is and how to recognize its outward symptoms, you can begin to learn how to control it and how to use it to improve your speeches.

In order to control stress and increase your confidence before an audience, you must learn to control both the physical factors and the emotional factors concerning the stressor.

Control Over Physical Factors

Dress

One of the simplest and most effective ways of building self-confidence in public speaking is to dress well and comfortably for the engagement. You're sure to feel better about yourself and this will help you perform better. Dress seems to make a difference to audiences, too. They are more attentive to a speaker who dresses neatly and appropriately.

Exercise

Much of the emotional tension in your body gets deposited in your muscles. Regular exercise can relieve your muscles of much of the daily stress in your life. You'll feel fitter, sleep better, and look healthier--and all these factors will add to your self-esteem and help you perform more effectively.

A little light exercise before a speaking engagement helps relieve muscles of physical stress brought on by speech anxiety. Try spending a few minutes privately limbering up with some non-strenuous stretching or **isometric exercises**.

Biofeedback

With training and practice, you can control negative physical responses to stress through biofeedback. This technique teaches you to control normally involuntary or unconscious body processes by making them evident through concentration. You can learn to sense your heart rate, body temperature, and blood pressure and then modify them through a conscious effort.

Familiarity with the Audience

Since you are more relaxed before an audience you know, try to reduce your fear of an unknown audience by getting to know them before the presentation. Welcome people individually as they enter the room, or sit in the audience and talk to people around you before you are called upon to speak. Even casually meeting a few listeners can greatly reduce your tension.

Breathing and Delivery Techniques

Stuttering and stammering is caused by running out of air, and much of the jerky delivery so common with stutterers is due to an inconsistent release of air past the **vocal cords**. To reduce this problem, modify your breathing by practising this technique. Try to increase the amount of air in your lungs without quite filling them, then slowly and steadily release the air from your lungs via the **trachea** while you are speaking.

Practise speaking in front of a mirror. Paying attention to your chest and your lips can help correct irregular breathing and poor **articulation**. You can work to improve your facial expression and eye contact, and can also look for any inadequacies in gesture and posture. Don't try to correct everything at once. Concentrate on one adjustment at a time.

Mnemonic Devices

Are you worried about opening your mouth to speak--and forgetting everything you were going to say? Proper preparation can help you relax and cope better with the threat of memory loss. An alternative to visual aids is to use **mnemonic devices**, such as symbols or **anagrams**, to call up key points and jog your memory while you're speaking.

Other minor afflictions

Simple techniques will help deal with other minor symptoms. Sucking a candy before speaking stimulates saliva production and counters a dry mouth. Holding a napkin in each hand for the first few minutes of the speech will counter damp palms. Non-prescriptive antacids may be the solution to your acidic stomach.

Control over Emotional Factors

Preparation

There's nothing worse than waiting to speak before a crowd when you don't feel you've really prepared enough. Once you're speaking, your self-doubt can make you seem tentative and indecisive. Again, perhaps the single most effective way of combatting speech anxiety is solid preparation--from the speech outline to a rehearsal, which will ensure that you've included all the pertinent information in your speech and that you've thought out its delivery. Solid preparation will also allow you to concentrate more on the material and less on the audience. With a thorough knowledge of your material, you will give a more relaxed and confident presentation, which will benefit speaker and audience alike.

Visualization

Visualization is a useful tool for all speakers. Find a quiet place where you can be alone before your presentation. Mentally run through your speech and anticipate any trouble spots. This forethought can help you overcome potential problems before they arise. Visualizing an assured, effective, and successful speech can bolster your confidence during the actual delivery.

Audience Desensitization

Those who feel a moderate degree of speech stress when talking in front of a crowd, can benefit from a technique called **audience desensitization**. You'll need a group of friends to help you out. Begin your speech with just one person in the room. At 30-second intervals, have additional listeners enter the room. This gradual increase in audience size should be barely perceptible to you. After ten minutes, you'll be speaking comfortably to twenty people.

Systematic Desensitization

If you experience a high degree of speech anxiety, you may wish to try **systematic desensitization** therapy with a professional. During this therapy, you relax various muscle groups and then visualize increasingly challenging speaking situations. This is an ongoing therapy and often a lengthy one. Whenever there's a significant rise in your stress level, systematic desensitization is reintroduced until you can visualize and "experience" success.

Videotaping Deliveries

For most speakers, one of the biggest worries is appearing nervous when giving a speech. One effective way of conquering this fear is to watch yourself speaking. Borrow a videotape camera and playback unit, and have someone film you while you speak. Most people think they look and sound much worse than they actually do when speaking. Watching yourself in action on videotape will help you identify areas for improvement and will highlight the strengths of your performance.

Confronting anxieties

What worries you most about public speaking? List your answers in ascending order of magnitude. Once these fears are written down, do something about them. Start with the easy ones. If you are tired and irritable before delivering a speech, try to get more sleep. A change in wardrobe might help you to be less self-conscious while on stage.

Once your minor anxieties have been addressed, confront the more serious ones. If temporary memory loss remains a continuing problem, develop mnemonic devices to better stimulate your memory under stress. If anxiety triggers attacks of hyperventilation, try inhaling and exhaling slowly and regularly into a paper bag to control breathing. If you're still concerned about appearing nervous to the audience, watch yourself in a mirror or on videotape. Ask friends for their honest opinions.

There are coping mechanisms for every symptom of stress. Experiment to determine which ones work most effectively for you.

CHAPTER 2

Nonverbal Communication

- Voice
- Body Language
- Using Nonverbal Communication

When you get up in front of an audience and speak, your main goal is communication. You have something to tell the audience and your spoken message is your primary message. But when speaking in public, you communicate with a lot more than just words. You're also sending out secondary messages by using **body language** and **voice**--the *way* you say something--to communicate nonverbally. Both primary and secondary messages work together as a complete communication package. They include information and directions for the listener on how to interpret that information.

Good listeners will try to get a full understanding of your message. They'll look beyond your words for other clues to help them understand what you're saying. They'll automatically appraise you so they can determine how to use your covert secondary messages to interpret your overt message. This is why the initial moments of any presentation are always so important. The audience is scrutinizing the speaker intensely to form an impression that will help it understand the message better.

Understanding nonverbal communication begins at an early age as part of our language training. Infants cannot understand the verbal messages of their parents until they have reached a **cognitive** stage in their language development. But they do react to nuances in intonation and facial expression--and they continue to do so throughout childhood and beyond. We learn to respond to and interpret the nonverbal images and sounds we encounter every time we interact with others or are exposed to media such as television.

The study of nonverbal communication has yielded a relatively new field of scholarship: **paralanguage**, a word incorporating the Greek prefix *para*, meaning "beyond," and referring to the study of influences that transcend everyday language. Paralanguage focuses on the study of two distinct language segments--**paralinguistics**, concerning verbal linguistics, and **kinesics**, concerning body language. Research shows that the combined delivery of paralinguistics and kinesics accounts for a significant portion of the message received by the listener. The listener who concentrates solely upon the worded message misses the secondary messages or instructions and, as a result, doesn't fully comprehend the complete message.

Paralanguage is culturally specific. Different cultures and subcultures have their own "rules" governing how a message is delivered orally. Mediterranean cultures rely heavily upon gesture as a visual instruction, while northern European cultures depend more upon **inflections** as voice instructions.

This can make it challenging for people from different cultures to communicate. Although most of the problems that arise during cross-cultural communication are language-related, a large proportion of misunderstandings can be attributed to misinterpretation of paralanguage.

North Americans, for example, are taught from an early age that eye contact is desirable during interpersonal communication. An inability or unwillingness to maintain eye contact during conversation signifies dishonesty or weakness of character. Japanese children, however, are taught not to establish eye contact, for looking down while addressing someone in their culture indicates respect.

So one of the keys to being a successful communicator is being able to interpret others' paralanguage correctly--and learning to control your own paralanguage. If you can control your own delivery, you can better control the audience's response to your message.

This chapter examines the components of voice and body language and how they can be interpreted and controlled in a presentational context.

Voice

Have you ever heard yourself on tape and thought, "I sound like *that*?" It's not often that we actually pay much attention to our voices. Physiology to an extent determines how you sound when speaking. The length and thickness of your vocal cords are contributing factors to your vocal pitch. The structure of your oral cavity and teeth affects your ability to articulate sounds. The size and configuration of your sinus cavities determines the degree of nasality in your speech.

Paralinguistics, on the other hand, concentrates on how the voice is influenced by *non*-physiological factors, such as volume, rate, pitch, and tone. These are aspects you can modify--and it is worth spending time working on it. The way a message *sounds* determines how the audience will interpret and react to it. Even minor changes in the paralinguistic presentation of a message can significantly alter its message to the audience. With practice, you can learn to exercise considerable control over your voice and, consequently, over your audience.

Volume

Volume, or loudness, is often a problem with inexperienced speakers. An overly loud voice can be irritating to listen to and sound brash or autocratic. Audiences don't like being yelled at. A speaker with an overly soft voice is equally distracting. Not only is it difficult to hear and understand, but the audience might conclude that it's listening to a reluctant speaker, and will soon lose patience and interest.

Some speakers begin at a normal volume but end up in a whisper. This problem of vocal drop-off is usually a product of nervousness, when the speaker either runs out of air while delivering a particularly long sentence, or prematurely focuses on the next sentence.

You can learn to *use* volume by varying it to periodically recapture your audience's attention. If you maintain a constant volume throughout the presentation, you will fail to distinguish the main points in your speech. Modulate your volume appropriately and it can serve as a voice clue, helping the audience identify your key points.

Rate

The rate or speed at which you deliver a speech can indicate to the audience how you feel about your material. A deliberate, plodding delivery often indicates solemnity or seriousness; a quickened pace suggests urgency or enthusiasm. Of course, speed of delivery varies from speaker to speaker, but most North Americans speak at a rate of around 160 words per minute.

Varying the delivery speed of different parts of your speech can help you highlight the main ideas and will influence listeners' subconscious interpretation of your message. A modulated delivery is less predictable, and will hold your listeners' interest by requiring them to actively vary their responses.

If you want to elicit a serious response, deliver your speech at a slower than average tempo. This gives the audience more time to consider the impact of each word. But don't keep the delivery plodding for too long, as it is also less challenging for the audience and increases the likelihood that it will become distracted.

Increase the tempo to suggest excitement or informality. But remember that although a fast delivery will initially stimulate an audience, you shouldn't try to maintain that excitement indefinitely. Keep the audience on its toes by once again modulating delivery speed.

Pitch

Vocal pitch is another important variable. The pitch of your voice is very difficult to control without practice, and this makes it a highly accurate verbal indicator of how you feel about the subject you are presenting.

The hardest time to control the pitch of your voice is at the beginning of your speech. Most public speakers--whether novices or experts--begin their speeches at a higher that normal pitch because the speech stress they are experiencing tenses and tightens their vocal cords so that they vibrate at a higher frequency. With relaxation, the vocal cords relax and assume their normal tension.

However, if you are excited or passionate about your subject, you'll likely have difficulty masking your emotions--and the pitch of your voice will be raised. A high pitch indicates emotional engagement. If you're also speaking quickly, the combination usually indicates your stress level is elevated. Although you may worry that you sound nervous or anxious, the audience will interpret the **intonation** shifts as vocal prompts.

Inflection plays a crucial role in your delivery. The list below demonstrates how moving the emphasis from word to word in a sentence can produce distinctly different meanings.

Why don't you ask him?

Why *don't* you ask him?

Why don't *you* ask him?

Why don't you *ask* him?

Why don't you ask *him*?

These five versions of the same sentence demonstrate various degrees of curiosity, impatience, and sarcasm. Every day you use inflection to convey subtle shades of meaning without even thinking about it. But do you use it in your public speaking? Appropriate inflection is a common casualty of speech anxiety. Tension can cause your vocal cords to be too tight to follow the natural rhythms of language. As a result, your performance can be monotonous and uninspiring.

Nervousness can give your sentences an upward intonation, with each one sounding like a question in a forced, unsynchronized over-inflection that results in a bewildering melody.

The stress reducing techniques referred to in the first chapter of this book can be helpful here. Practise controlling speech inflection so you can make it an effective part of your public speaking.

Tone

A speech on ballet delivered in a gruff, husky tone, or a speech on military strategy delivered in a breathy tone, would immediately sound incongruous. What's behind this stereotypical response? Tone refers to the general characteristics of your voice and their effects upon an audience. The tonal qualities of your voice significantly affect how your message will be received, often overriding the message itself, because listeners automatically associate these qualities with personality. After years of cultural conditioning, listeners expect you to sound the way you look and to employ a tone of voice that is somehow commensurate with your subject. If your tone isn't what the listeners expect, then much of your initial message will be lost until they adjust.

Tones range from nasal to breathy and from hoarse to flat and convey an infinite variety of impressions--harsh, excited, bored, angry, amused, apologetic, sexy, conceited. Vocal tone is the result of a combination of factors, most notably linked to physiology and breathing patterns.

Since you can't change your physiology, if you want to modify your tone of voice, it is necessary to concentrate on changing your breathing patterns. Practise steadily releasing the air from your lungs while you talk. This is the simplest and most effective way of achieving a consistent and acceptable vocal tone.

Body Language

Body language, or kinesics, is the way in which you communicate physically, especially in combination with speech. Your body language provides an audience with clues or instructions on how to interpret the oral message. And as with verbal communication, body language can validate or contradict the oral message. Since most people are visually oriented, your audience will usually be more aware of your body language than of the secondary messages sent by your voice.

Dress, gesture, visual contact, and **proxemics**, or the amount of space you keep between yourself and your audience, are culturally based factors that influence the interpretation of body language. Posture, movement, and facial expression are factors that are more expressive of individual personality.

As a novice public speaker, you are probably all too well aware of your body language. It is quite natural to feel awkward and self-conscious standing before an audience. The danger is in letting this discomfort undermine your rapport with the audience.

There are techniques in using dress, visual contact, posture, and gesture to modify and control your body language and present a positive visual image to your audience.

Dress

Dress is the physical element in communication that is both the most obvious to an audience and the easiest to modify. Although continued acceptance will depend upon your performance and experience, your appearance will help to determine whether an audience accepts you initially. As soon as you step onto the stage, the audience will immediately evaluate you on the basis of your appearance, including the colour and style of your clothes and your grooming. How you dress tells them what you think about yourself and how you want to be thought of by them. A sloppy or unkempt appearance usually indicates a careless attitude or low self-esteem. On the other hand, an exaggerated display of grooming and dress may suggest self-importance or vanity.

The audience will pay special attention to the colour of your clothing. At formal presentations your appearance will be expected to reflect that formality. Black, grey, or navy blue clothes are traditionally worn at formal gatherings and they lend a conservativeness to your visual impression. At informal gatherings, less staid colours are acceptable. Avoid wildly colourful clothes whatever the occasion, because they will divert attention from what you are saying.

Clothing style is subject to the same restrictions as colour. The style should be appropriate to the subject of the presentation, the occasion, and the audience. If your appearance departs radically from what the audience would expect, it risks distracting the audience from your words and making them uncomfortable. To reduce the chances of alienating your listeners before you even open your mouth, follow this rule of thumb: wear what the audience does.

Don't forget to evaluate your clothing accessories. Again, if they are gaudy or inappropriate, they'll shift too much of the audience's attention from your message, and produce a contradictory visual message. For example, if you are discussing the plight of the homeless, you may not be very convincing if you are dripping with expensive rings and jewellery. Aim to gain audience confidence by co-ordinating your visual message with your verbal one.

Visual Contact

The most prominent of all the physical factors governing paralanguage is eye contact. Of course, it is most influential at close quarters during interpersonal communication when the eyes can be clearly seen. The slightest nuances indicated by subtle changes in lid movement and eye position can signify major shifts in meaning. Our culture prizes face-to-face communication because, ostensibly, it lends itself to honesty and accuracy. And it is the eyes which tell the listener the most.

But visual contact is also essential in a public speaking forum. Even where the speaker's eye movements aren't obvious to people far behind the first few rows, your audience will be uncannily aware of visual contact. It will enhance its interpretation of your material by watching your eyes, and you will be able to gauge the audience's reaction to what you are saying by watching it. The visual bond you form with your audience does much to establish trust and a rapport between you. Not only does it make *you* more comfortable, but visual contact also puts the audience at ease and makes it more receptive to your message.

In fact, at least 90 percent of your time on stage should be spent looking at the audience, with no more than 10 percent of the time spent consulting notes. Frequently referring to notes will make you appear nervous and unsure, and will deprive the audience of the clues provided by visual contact and facial expression.

If you are inexperienced, it might be tempting to limit your field of vision to the first few rows of listeners, especially in a darkened auditorium where most of the audience is invisible. But it's not enough simply to look at the same people throughout your whole speech. Look, or appear to look, at everyone so that you avoid alienating sections of the audience. **Pan** the audience, periodically stopping your eye motion at various points in the room. This will give the impression that you are personally addressing everyone.

Facial Expression

With a simple glance at your expression the audience will probably have a good idea of how you feel about your subject, your listeners, and yourself. Many people consider the eyes the most striking feature of the face, so eye contact is a critical component of facial expression. Because of the configuration of the facial muscles, the muscles around the eyes work in tandem with those of the rest of the face. Spend some time looking in a mirror and you will see how your eyes appear to mimic your mouth and emphasize your thoughts or feelings. Grin broadly and you'll see your eyes become elongated on the horizontal axis, making them appear to smile. Open your mouth to register shock or surprise and your cheek muscles lower, elongating your eyes on the vertical axis and causing them to show surprise. A half-smile or a sneer will automatically raise your cheek and brow on one side of your face to heighten the effect of your mouth.

Your facial musculature also influences your expression. Fatty tissue in your face, such as wrinkles and dimples, is manipulated by the muscles to produce uniquely personal expressions.

An effective speaker's face will naturally register a range of emotions as the speech progresses--and they can range widely, from anger and sorrow to joy and doubt. It is, however, virtually impossible to practise using facial expressions to engage the audience, for the very reason that the expressions that make the greatest impact upon an audience are those that are natural and unplanned--expressions that appear only when you are relaxed and focused on your subject. Work on remaining calm, and your face will do the rest naturally.

Posture and Movement

You step onto the stage and for the first few minutes of your speech, you stand rigidly, trying to remember those initial paragraphs, trying to control your perspiring hands. "A-ha," think the people in the audience. "A beginner."

Clues such as your posture and movement, or lack of it, help audiences to size you up initially, especially when people far from the stage can't see your facial expressions and gestures clearly. Are you standing or leaning? Erect or slouched? Able to come out from behind the podium or frozen behind it? These visual hints indicate to the audience your degree of comfort and control.

Much has been written about the ideal posture for a public speaker. The traditional advice is to place the feet apart, stand erect, square the shoulders, and push out the chest. Such an uncomfortable position becomes even more so when you try to move, and what should be natural movements end up looking robot-like and contrived.

Posture and movement should reflect confidence and personality. By allowing freer rein to your emotions, you appear more relaxed and natural. Begin as soon as you walk to the podium, as audiences will be drawing their first perceptions about you then. Don't saunter or shuffle or you'll appear reluctant; stride confidently and purposefully to the podium and the audience will know you are eager and prepared to speak.

Once on stage, don't confine yourself to the podium. Audiences may expect you to spend most of your time there, but they are perfectly capable of visually tracking you as you move about. The podium should be considered your "home base," because it serves as the focal point for speaker and audience alike. But try to incorporate the movements you would normally use in a one-on-one conversation. Such movements are especially convincing if you move for specific purposes. Moving toward the audience to better hear a question, moving to turn on an overhead projector, or heading to the blackboard so you can write on it all fall into the category of purposeful movement.

However, too much motion can be as distracting as a total lack of movement, since there is a danger of your movements receiving more attention than your message. Follow your natural inclinations with respect to movement, but adjust the amount and speed of motion if you feel your movements are erring toward either extreme.

The most effective movements in terms of audience control are the finer movements. Placing one foot ahead of the other and bending the knee or placing one hand in a pocket conveys a relaxed attitude that puts the audience at ease. Taking a step or two away from the podium before the introduction of each new presentation segment serves as a visual **transitional device**, allowing the audience to better follow your verbal message. Taking a step or two toward the audience signals an important point in your speech.

Remember that the key to the effective use of posture and movement is moderation and spontaneity. By incorporating consistent movements as visual signals and avoiding predictably rhythmic motions, you can maintain your audience's interest and attention.

Gesture

Gestures--movements of the arms, hands, fingers, and other parts of the body designed to denote context and meaning--are another form of body language to consider when public speaking. Wide, sweeping gestures are termed **gross**; the subtler ones are called **fine** gestures. Generally, you use a combination of gross and fine gestures during the course of a presentation.

Unlike fidgets or twitches, gestures are not the product of nervousness or anxiety. They are performed with a specific purpose: to clarify the spoken message.

Audiences can usually differentiate between true gestures and nervous movements, because gestures should relate directly to what you're saying at that moment. When you point an index finger directly at the audience during a motivational speech, you are performing a gesture; when you unconsciously rearrange speech notes, you are not. Nonetheless, both motions convey a message. The first tells the audience that the point you're making is an important one; the second conveys anxiety or discomfort.

Gross gestures employing the arms and other parts of the body often describe the size, shape, or location of the subject discussed. Use them to inform your audience of a major concept. Use fine gestures of the hands and fingers to convey subtleties concerned with matters of degree or attitude. Fine gestures are more suggestive than gross gestures and will gently underscore your verbal message. Paradoxically, fine gestures can have a greater impact upon the audience than the more dramatic gross gestures. Especially if you overuse your gross gestures and they lose their impact. As with all kinesics, moderate use increases the impact of the gesture.

Some of the most telling gestures do not accompany verbal messages. When you bow your head, shrug your shoulders, or cross your arms, you speak volumes to the audience. And just as well-timed and appropriately long pauses can increase the impact of your spoken word, so unaccompanied gestures can have the same effect.

Gestures are most believable when they are spontaneous and natural. Premeditated gestures rarely gain the audience's confidence. They will simply appear contrived. The novice speaker should try not to concentrate too much on gestures, but rather let them occur naturally as the speech unfolds.

An important point to consider when you are addressing members of other cultural groups is that gestures can signify different feelings or ideas in different cultures. Pointing at the audience might be considered rude in some cultures, so do some gesture research before making your speech.

Proxemics

The next time you enter an elevator with strangers, take a look at how the passengers distance themselves from one another. The study of personal, interpersonal, and group space as it relates to communication is called **proxemics**. The physical distances people keep between each other during communication indicate the quality and nature of that communication.

Most people use distance as an unconscious defence mechanism or social barrier to help them interact at a mutually comfortable remove. Distance can also reflect status and maintain control. In a formal one-on-one meeting, the physical barrier between people of different status imposed by a desk is an effective distancing control. A distance of about two meters separates people in this situation, a distance that the controller can choose to maintain or decrease by remaining behind the desk or moving out and sitting closer to the other.

As familiarity increases, we draw closer together. We tend to communicate with one another at a distance of a little over half a meter. This distance allows us to use and respond to the full range of facial expressions and gestures, and the result is immediate and accurate communication.

The most intimate proxemic distance is anything less than about half a meter and often includes physical contact. The decision to communicate at these close quarters must be a mutual one and is reserved for those who are very familiar with each other. When we find strangers within our intimate spatial range, such as on a crowded elevator or a subway, we can feel uncomfortable, with a more or less conscious desire to increase the spatial buffer zone between us and others. In other cultures, where crowding is an everyday reality, people tend to be less **territorial** and protective of their personal space.

Physical objects and their positioning within the sphere of communication also influence proxemics and behaviour patterns. How we react to physical objects in social situations indicates our willingness to communicate with others as well as the level at which we wish to communicate. In an airport lounge or bus terminal, people will rarely choose to sit right next to one another, unless all the other seats are taken. Even people arriving early at a meeting will rarely choose the seat next to the one reserved for the Chairperson. On the other hand, those on intimate terms will often choose to sit beside one another.

Of course, other factors can influence spatial positioning and force people to interact at uncomfortable distances. For example, ambient noise may force strangers closer together so they can hear each other. But they will probably only remain at that distance long enough to complete their interchange before moving apart to a more comfortable distance.

One way to use a knowledge of proxemics in a public speaking situation is to try to develop a sense of familiarity with the audience by closing the physical gap between you. You'll appear less removed and inaccessible if you move from behind the podium toward the front of the stage, and this can improve your rapport with the audience. Even if it only brings you a meter or so closer to the front row, the entire audience will appreciate your symbolic gesture.

CHAPTER 3

Visual Aids

- Types of Visual Aids
- Types of Visual Media
- Choosing Visual Aids
- Using Visual Aids

Your speech is ready--and it sounds great to you, but you still have reservations. How can you really grab your audience's attention so that it will take in what you are saying and remember it after you've finished?

Most people learn least effectively by listening. Combine that with the modern audience's extremely limited attention span and you're right not to expect it to both comprehend and remember the material you present orally. People assimilate more information by listening and seeing, and learn best by listening and doing.

The answer to making a presentation memorable is to incorporate visual aids or interactive demonstrations. Properly constructed and effectively presented, visuals accompanying an oral delivery promote understanding, maintain interest, and aid retention of the material presented.

Visual aids are most effective when they are audience-centred, created for one purpose--to enhance the audience's comprehension of integral concepts or ideas. They should be simple and clear, so they can be fully understood at a glance. Title and label them clearly so the audience is immediately aware of what it is looking at.

Presenting visual aids effectively can be a challenge. A presenter with a barrage of visual aids who leafs rapidly through a flip chart, races through a series of overheads, then moves to the chalkboard to illustrate further arguments will leave the audience reeling. Trying to listen *and* take notes will be frustrating. An overwhelming amount of information presented in a brief time and resulting in decreased comprehension is called **information overload**.

The cardinal rule when using visual aids is *keep them to a minimum*. Timing is important too. Present visuals when they relate directly to your verbal message, just as figures in a textbook are designed to illustrate the written material on the same page. Show a series of overheads pivotal to audience comprehension as your speech concludes and you are picking a time when the attention of the audience is lowest. The length of time you devote to showing visual aids is also an important factor in their effectiveness. Remove them too soon and they will not have been fully digested by the viewers. Displaying visuals that no longer relate to your changing verbal message can confuse the audience.

Consider carefully whether the type of presentation you are going to give will indeed benefit from visual support. Not all presentations do. Special occasion speeches such as eulogies, speeches of introduction, and pep talks work best unadorned, since the message relies upon the situation and the associated atmosphere for much of its impact.

Here are some key questions to help you consider the use of visual aids when preparing for a presentation:

1. *Is the visual aid necessary?* Quite often, the orally presented material is clear enough to be understood without further visual assistance. This is an important consideration when attempting to limit the number of visuals in the presentation.

2. *Is the visual aid relevant?* If the aid doesn't relate directly to the verbal message, it will be counterproductive and only confuse listeners.

3. *Is the choice of visual aid the best one?* With an increasingly wide range of visuals available, making the right choice is difficult. Explore all the various options.

4. *Is the visual aid clear?* Unless the message conveyed is unmistakable, it will have failed. A clear visual aid is simple, uncluttered, and legible. If the audience must spend its time deciphering the visual, the oral message will be missed.

5. *Is the visual aid aesthetically appealing?* People react positively to an aesthetically pleasing visual aid that is neat, eye-catching, and well-organized.

Visual aids should be simple to produce. If they take a lot of time and effort, the energy might have been better spent on your speech. Also consider how portable they are and how long they will take to set up.

Think carefully before using an audio aid as an adjunct to your oral presentation. Instrumental background music can work well to establish an atmosphere during your visual presentation, but in general, audio aids such as tape-recordings tend to distract audiences, and the taped voice interrupts the **cadence** and flow established by your voice.

A Closer Look at Visual Aids

Visual aids can be classified in two ways: by type--that is, the image or graphic chosen--and by medium of presentation, or method of delivery. The combination of visual types and media offers you a variety of formats to choose from.

Types of Visual Aids

It is important to choose the types of presentation aid that best suit your specific purpose. If you are presenting statistical information, the logical option is one of a variety of graphs: line, bar, pie, or pictographs. If you have a large amount of information that requires a concise visual summary, charts provide you with the best graphic capability. Geographic location and relation is obviously most effectively illustrated by maps. Photographs are your best choice when dealing with works of art and specific objects. Information concerning organization, structure, or relatedness is best indicated by flow charts or schematics. Explaining mechanical construction and operation may best be using cut-away drawings or cross-sections. Three-dimensional objects and models may also be considered, although their size may limit their usefulness to a small audience situation.

Graphs

Graphs are an excellent way to demonstrate statistical data, trends, and proportions. The most commonly employed graph is the **line graph** (Fig. 3.1); it usually incorporates time and units to chart a trend. Convention dictates that time is always indicated on the horizontal or **x-axis** while other units are displayed on the vertical or **y-axis**. Line graphs can be extremely useful when you require significant detail and accuracy.

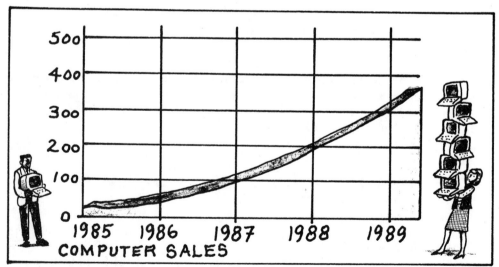

Fig. 3.1   Line Graph

Be aware, though, that graphs can become confusing. Try not to chart too many trends on the same graph. Generally, no more than three lines should appear on a single line graph. If you must chart more than one trend on a graph, keep each line distinct from the others by using different colours or print patterns. Include a **key** on the graph to explain what the various lines represent.

Although **bar graphs** are not as accurate as line graphs, they will provide your presentation with a greater visual impact. You can use them to encourage visual comparisons by illustrating general trends in a dramatic and easily understood style. While most bar graphs incorporate the two axes found in line graphs, the bars can originate from either axis (Figs. 3.2, 3.3). Nonetheless, whenever you want to show time or distance, place these variables on the horizontal or x-axis, where the audience will expect to find them. If the bars are wide enough, mark concise labels or unit measures on them.

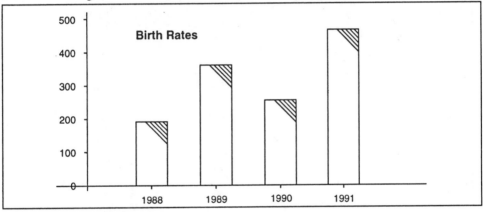

Figure 3.2   Vertical Bar Graph

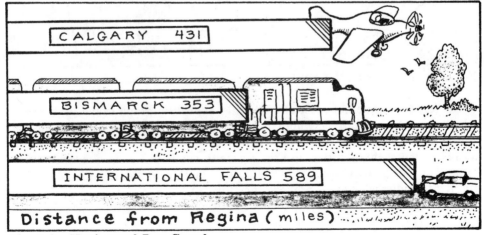

Fig. 3.3   Horizontal Bar Graph

As with line graphs, keep your bar graphs simple and uncluttered. Separate the bars by white space to make them easy to understand, and don't overwhelm the audience with the number of bars on the graph.

The third type of graph used as a presentation aid is the **pie graph**, which is based on a circle, portions or slices of which represent a percentage of the whole. The pie graph is useful for demonstrating relationships between seg-mented portions of the whole by offering comparisons based on relative size. If one particular segment of the whole serves as the basis for your presentation, lift or **explode** this portion to effectively highlight the presentation's focus (Fig. 3.4). Don't indicate too many slices or the pie graph will lose its effectiveness. Limiting it to a few large slices will aid viewer interpretation and let you include percentages in the portions.

Fig. 3.4   Exploded Pie Graph

The least accurate but most aesthetically appealing graph is the **pictograph**, which uses representative symbols or figures from your discussion to illustrate comparisons. These representations can be used in two ways. The most accurate means of representation is to use the figure to symbolize a set number of units, established in a key (Fig. 3.5). The second method is to vary the size of the figures to indicate relative proportions (Fig. 3.6). While not as accurate, this does dramatically illustrate the comparisons. Remember to choose simple and relevant symbols for your pictograph.

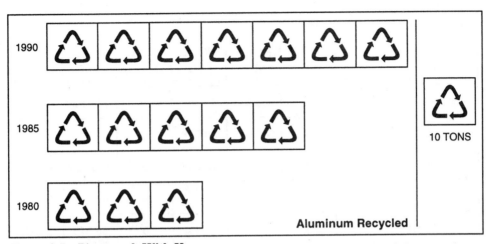

Figure 3.5   Pictograph With Key

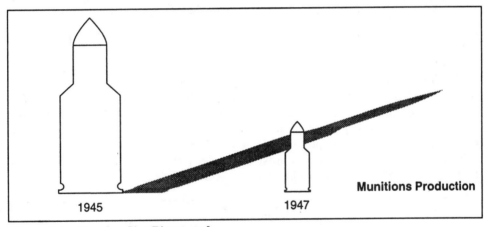

Figure 3.6   Varying Size Pictograph

Charts

Charts vary in design and function, but they share one important feature: they present a large volume of related material in a limited space. The most commonly used charts are **summary charts**, which provide key points in an easily digestible word form (Fig. 3.7). They are especially valuable when illustrating comparisons between like objects, allowing viewers to discern similarities and differences at a glance. Summary charts are also useful for demonstrating the essential steps of a process. Number and present the point-form steps in chronological order to clarify their presentation. Using the chart effectively takes practice. Reveal the information on the chart one point at a time to prevent your viewers from reading too far ahead.

Great Lakes League Attendance						
TEAM	HOME DATES	HOME ATT.	HOME AVG.	ROAD DATES	ROAD ATT.	ROAD AVG.
BUFFALO	3	130,084	43,361	3	149,108	49,703
CLEVELAND	6	148,548	24,758	0	—	—
HAMILTON	3	36,293	12,098	3	130,084	43,361
MILWAUKEE	0	—	—	6	186,029	31,005
TORONTO	3	121,925	40,642	3	68,975	22,992
WINDSOR	6	208,636	34,773	0	—	—

Figure 3.7   Summary Chart

A chart can also be presented in graphic form. **Organization charts** display hierarchies and organizational structures (Fig. 3.8). The most important or powerful elements are placed at the top, with the influence moving in a downward pattern. To explain a complex process or relationship, a **flow chart** is useful. This is a diagram that outlines a logical sequence from a starting point through to an end point. Mechanical processes are best indicated in **schematic charts**. Schematics most often show the relationships between interconnecting elements in mechanical or electronic devices.

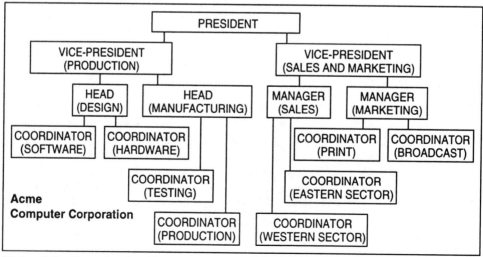

Figure 3.8   Organization Chart

Cross Sections

If your presentation discusses the construction of a mechanical device, consider representing this by cross-section or cut-away illustrations (Fig. 3.9). These can be used to show the interior view of the device along either the vertical or horizontal axis. If a portion of the object is the focus of your discussion, lift or explode it from the rest of your graphic to highlight its importance.

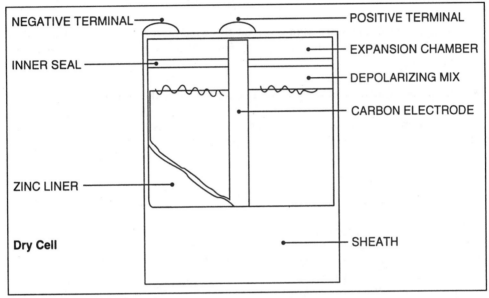

Figure 3.9   Cross Section

Maps

It will come as no surprise that the best visual reference when your topic of discussion is a geographic area is a map. Maps are extremely adaptable visual aids. You can map a specific area to indicate any one of a number of different features. The detail indicated is determined by scale.

The map can display either natural features or political divisions. **Physical maps** show the physical features of a specific region, such as mountains, valleys, or rivers. **Relief maps** indicate these features by using different colours or shading. **Contour maps** (Fig. 3.10) also show elevations and depressions by using unbroken lines (contours) that join points of the same elevation. Weather maps may also employ this principle, with areas experiencing the same temperature or barometric pressure joined by **isotherms** and **isobars**.

If your speech is dealing with political boundaries, such as national, state, or provincial borders, you may wish to use a **political map** (Fig. 3.11) as a visual aid, with each area being highlighted in a different colour.

Here are some quick tips to maps:

• Unless otherwise indicated, north is aligned with the top of the map.

• Contours, isotherms, and isobars never intersect.

• Relief map colours are standardized the world over (on a graduated scale, deep browns indicate high elevations; deep greens indicate low features).

• Distance is always indicated by a scale found at the bottom of the map.

Avoid maps that are too detailed to use as visual aids. They should only show the features that relate directly to your presentation.

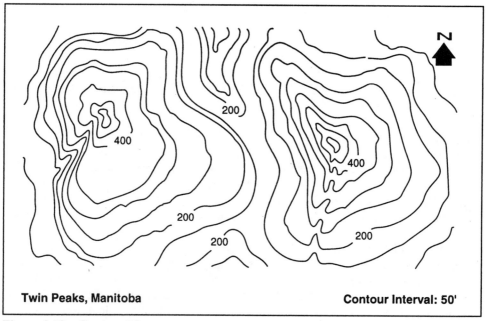

Figure 3.10   Contour Map

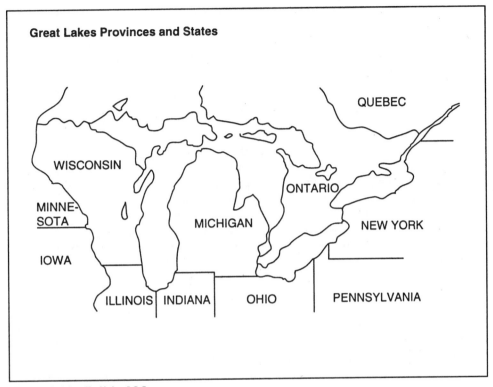

Figure 3.11   Political Map

Photographs

Photographs can be a great visual support, and the availability of high quality and inexpensive photo reproduction services has increased their use. You can have a high resolution photograph enlarged to a size appropriate for a small group presentation relatively inexpensively. It is also inexpensive to convert photographs into slides or overhead transparencies for high quality reproduction.

Types of Visual Media

Once you decide on the type of visual support you want to use during your presentation, it's time to think about the form in which you will present it. There are many choices to consider, including objects and models, the chalkboard, the flip chart, enlargements, projection devices, and handouts. Here is a quick guide to some of their strengths and weaknesses:

Objects and Models

Objects can be excellent visual supports if your presentation is for a small audience. The object can be circulated so audience members get an exact impression of its size, shape, mass, and colour.

If the object itself is too large to be transported to and from a presentation, one solution is to use a model. Scale models are exact replicas of the objects they represent. Constructed to scale, they still convey an accurate impression of the original. If you are discussing a working mechanical object, such as a steam engine, presenting a miniature **working model** as a visual aid will help your audience see how it really works. Working models are usually constructed to scale, but they have the added advantage of being fully or partially operational. They can, however, be expensive or difficult to construct, and like objects, the size of most models limits their usefulness to small audience situations.

Chalkboard

A common mistake is to rely on the chalkboard during your presentation just because it is readily available in most classrooms and seminar rooms. The chalkboard is not an effective visual support because you must leave the podium area to use it. Once at the board, you must turn your back on the audience to write or draw, and, because most speakers find it difficult to speak and write simultaneously, you probably won't talk much while you're at the board. As a result, you can alienate your audience and increase the risk of your message being misunderstood.

If the chalkboard is still the medium of choice as your primary visual support, it is best to prepare it ahead of time, although this also has drawbacks, since it allows viewers to jump ahead in your presentation. All in all, chalkboards are most effective as secondary visual aids, and it is best to use them sparingly and in support of another prepared visual aid.

Flip Chart

Many seminar rooms are equipped with a flip chart, usually positioned by the seminar leader's chair where it can be used during the **brainstorming** process. Ideas that arise out of the meeting can be quickly noted on the chart in full view of the meeting participants.

The flip chart shares a major disadvantage with the chalkboard--it, too, is difficult to see from a distance. You can, however, prepare a number of visuals for a flip chart in advance of your presentation without showing them prematurely.

The flip chart's other advantage is portability. It can be positioned near the podium, thereby eliminating excessive movement on stage.

Enlargements

For decades, photo enlargements have been a favourite method of presenting high quality/high impact graphics. Because they are used in large audience situations, the photographs are usually black and white, so they can be easily seen at a distance. Enlargements are popular in persuasive presentations to large audiences, such as at political conventions. Candidates often have enlargements of themselves positioned behind the podium, the photographs there to support the image they try to convey in their verbal messages.

The use of photo enlargements has declined significantly because of high production costs and the increasing popularity of projection devices, most notably 35 mm slides and overhead projections. The only significant advantage enlargements hold over slides and other projections is that they can be easily seen in a well lighted room.

Because of their high cost, enlargements might be reserved for use with speeches to be presented a number of times, the repeat performances offsetting the cost of production.

Projection Devices

The advent of high quality projection devices has revolutionized visual presentations. Their high definition, portability, and low cost mean that even amateur speakers can employ professional quality visual aids. Today, projectors are readily available in most presentation rooms.

But not all projectors are created equal, and there are some projection devices to avoid. A movie projector, for example, requires a darkened room, which would render you invisible to the audience. And even without an accompanying soundtrack, the noise a movie projector produces would make it difficult for you to be heard. It also can be costly, and requires a lot of effort to set up.

Videotape has all but replaced film. You'll find that videotape equipment is highly portable, requires significantly less effort and expertise to operate, and can be shown in a lighted room. Its only disadvantage is its projection size, since most video monitors are too small to be seen by large assemblies.

Another visual aid that has lost popularity is the 35 mm slide projector. Like film projectors, slide projectors require substantial preparation and set-up time. Slides must be loaded in the proper order and the lens focused. Again, your presentation must be made in the dark and over the noise of the slide projector.

Although they have a limited application and should be reserved for situations where their use is essential, slides probably remain your best choice for the presentation of high definition colour stills. They are particularly well suited for showing artwork and panoramic photographs because of their colour accuracy and contrast. Some computer software manufacturers have recently marketed graphics programs that create high quality laser slides, but these are only marginally better than laser overheads.

Of all the projection devices currently available, the opaque projector is undoubtedly the largest and most unwieldy. Its unique property is its ability to project any image off a page onto a screen. However, the quality of these images is often poor. Paper quality and positioning can create shadows, especially around the borders, significantly reducing its impact. Usually used to project a page from a book, the opaque image tends to be crowded and confusing to the viewer. Opaque projector usage has declined dramatically with the increasing popularity of overhead projectors.

It's no wonder the overhead projector is so popular. Transportation is not usually a problem, as it is a standard fixture in most presentation rooms. Overhead transparencies are extremely portable and, with a minimum of care, can last years. Transparency markers allow you to write on a blank or processed transparency while delivering your presentation. This means you can illustrate your speech without having to turn away from the audience. Overheads can be shown in a fully lighted room, allowing the audience to continue to follow your facial expressions and gestures clearly. So that your viewers don't read ahead of your presentation, you can block from the audience's view portions of the transparency not in use.

The image created by an overhead projector on a screen, especially when it is generated by a laser printer, rivals slides in clarity and definition. Recent developments in colour copying and transfer mean you can show inexpensive and effective colour transparencies.

Transparencies can be produced in a number of ways. You can transfer them from photocopies on most copy machines. Black and white photocopies can be transformed onto single colour heat-activated transparencies by using overhead heat transfers. Combine a series of these varied coloured overheads and you've got a coloured **overlay**--a high impact, professional multidimensional visual.

Handouts

Handouts are generally considered to be ineffective visual aids, primarily because they are often sources of distraction. When you pass out a handout, audience members will immediately focus on it and probably miss your next few points. For this reason, it is best to distribute any handouts after your presentation. Distribute handouts prior to a presentation only if you expect your listeners to write on them. When some speakers are teaching a difficult process, they write on processed transparencies and expect the audience to do the same on the handouts.

Handouts can take many forms. Bibliographies can direct listeners to publications related to the presentation topic. Written material too lengthy to be read or reviewed during the speech can be distributed for the audience to read at a later date. Challenging information and ideas delivered during a lecture can be summarized on a handout for study purposes.

The Speaker

Most of the above visual aids have the disadvantage of drawing attention away from you, the speaker. By giving a demonstration, or even wearing a visual aid, you remain the object of audience focus and interest. Demonstrations are dynamic and eye-catching, and can illustrate a process much more effectively than words. If you are discussing a dance step or a martial arts movement, a demonstration will be far more graphic and illuminating than any diagram. Similarly, if you are discussing a fashion item, the costume itself will better illustrate the colour, cut, and impact of the garment than any picture could.

The Audience

Whenever possible, include the audience in any explanation of a process. People learn best by doing. A diagram can help your listeners get a good idea of the intricacies of origami, the Japanese art of paper folding. Making a paper object for them will give them a better idea. But they will best understand the process if you provide them with paper and guide them through the steps themselves.

Using Visual Aids

A number of guidelines govern the effective use of presentation aids. The following suggestions ensure that the visual aids used will enhance, and not detract from, your oral presentation.

1. *Test visual aids for clarity.* Your visuals should be comprehensible without an accompanying verbal explanation. When preparing for the presentation, test your visual aids for clarity by asking friends unfamiliar with them to interpret them.

2. *Test visual aids immediately prior to the presentation.* Test mechanical and electrical visual devices, such as projection devices, to ensure they work properly.

3. *Use visual aids sparingly.* Overuse visuals and they'll lose their impact on viewers. Short presentations (seven minutes or less) should incorporate a maximum of two visuals.

4. *Keep visual aids simple.* Their purpose is to clarify or illustrate the verbal message. Complicated or complex visuals defeat that purpose.

5. *Don't show visual aids prematurely.* Audiences that see or read visuals before you refer to them often lose interest in the visual and the speech itself. This is especially true if you give the audience handouts prior to the presentation.

6. *Show visual aids only while you are referring to them.* Visuals that remain in view of the audience after the focus of the presentation has shifted will sometimes distract and confuse listeners. Only show aids long enough for the audience to understand them and their relationship to the speech.

7. *Make direct reference to visual aids.* Explain them to the audience at the appropriate times in the presentation, referring directly to them so the audience realizes how the visuals relate to your speech.

8. *Don't talk to the visual aids.* If you're inexperienced, you may be tempted to look at the visuals and not at the audience, especially when you use projection devices. It is important for you to maintain visual contact with listeners to gauge their response to the communication aids.

9. *Maintain visual aids.* If you're planning to reuse visual aids over a period of time, make sure they are maintained properly. Store slides and videotapes in dustproof cases; clean or reproduce overhead transparencies to ensure a sharp image.

CHAPTER 4

Adjudication: Evaluating the Presentation

- Individual versus Group Evaluation
- Evaluating Delivery
- Evaluating Content
- Judging General Effectiveness

To be successful, a speech must be compelling to listen to; it must hold the listeners' attention from beginning to end and leave them feeling like they've both enjoyed and benefitted from the experience. Bear in mind that speeches have two primary components--delivery and content--and that both are equally important. A presentation heavy on content but lacking a polished delivery will be ineffective; similarly, the slick delivery of a speech without substance will be valueless. The delivery should enhance, not detract from, the content of the presentation. The key, then, is to strive for a balance--a manageable, comprehensible text presented in a way that captures and maintains audience interest.

One way to learn how to give a great speech is to look at how speeches are evaluated. Rating the effectiveness of a presentation is not an easy task. An audience tends to evaluate a speech largely by "feel," making a subjective appraisal of the presentation as a whole. An **adjudicator** looks at the individual components of the speech. A familiarity with the components of an effective speech is useful to the individual speaker as well as the speaker who is part of a group.

Individual Evaluation

If you are being adjudicated as an individual speaker, you will be judged on your vocal and physical delivery and on the content of your presentation. The evaluation will encompass your entire presentation, from when you take the podium to how you handle the question and answer period. Specifically, the following elements will be examined:

Delivery (Vocal)

Projection

This refers to the force of your voice. You must speak at least at a minimum force that allows the listener furthest from you to hear each word clearly. Vary your **projection**. Increase it when a major point is made and revert to the previous level until your next major point. Properly used, projection is an effective control over the audience.

Pitch

Take care to avoid the common problem of sounding monotonous; varying the **pitch** of your voice maintains listener attention.   Modulate the pitch of your voice with the importance of the ideas or information you are presenting. In most instances, pitch should rise in tandem with projection for major points, and then drop back to its prior level. Pitch too, can be effectively used to influence the audience.

Articulation

Each syllable of each word you speak should be clearly articulated. Crispness and clarity of articulation allow the listener to clearly understand what's being said. Try to maintain crisp articulation and a good level of projection for the entirety of each sentence, and guard against vocal drop offs, common to many inexperienced speakers.

Pronunciation

The pronunciation of some words may pose a problem for you; practise and fully understand these words before you use them in a presentation. Pronunciation and accent vary from region to region. When regionalism becomes a factor, you should strive for a standard, dictionary pronunciation.

Timing

This term does not refer to the elapsed time of a speech, but rather the rate of delivery. The average delivery pace is about 160 words per minute. By varying the rate, you can place emphasis on specific portions of your presentation. By slowing down the delivery when making an important point, you can both recapture the audience's attention and ensure that it clearly hears what you are saying. Timing also includes the use of pauses. Pausing after an important statement lends it gravity and allows the audience time to ponder the information.

Delivery (Physical)

Posture

Good posture fulfills two functions: it creates a positive visual impression for the audience and it prevents speaker fatigue. But don't confuse good posture with a rigid stance. Practise developing a relaxed physical attitude that looks presentable and is comfortable. Avoid leaning against a wall or on a podium or lectern, however, as this leads to a number of other related problems. An acceptable position is one hand in your pocket and one knee slightly bent. If you appear relaxed and respectful of the audience, the audience will feel relaxed and be more receptive to your words.

Movement

Excessive movement is distracting to the audience, forcing it to both listen to you and visually track you across the stage. A good rule of thumb is to limit your sphere of movement to two steps in any direction from the lectern. On the other hand, if you don't move at all, you'll appear static. Keep your movements purposeful and fluid, not tentative or mechanical.

Gesture

Your gestures should complement your verbal message and thereby enhance comprehension. It's not a good idea to stand with your hands clasped behind your back, since you'll sacrifice a valuable way of giving added meaning to a point. Be wary of sending messages you don't intend: crossing your arms in front of you can make you appear argumentative and threatening.

As discussed in Chapter 2, **gestures** are classified as **fine** or **gross**. A fine gesture is subtle, such as the slight movement of your hand to emphasize a point. In most instances, this is all that is required to underscore the importance of what you are saying. A gross gesture is much more dramatic and usually involves the motion of your entire arm. While the gross gesture can be effective, overuse it and you diminish its impact. Keep your gestures looking natural and spontaneous.

Visual Contact

The most effective way to establish a rapport with your listeners is through visual contact. That's why you should never have a fully composed speech at hand. The temptation to read is too great, and pitch, timing, projection, and visual contact are usually compromised. Instead, use your eyes to make each member of the audience feel personally addressed by you. In a small group situation, look at each member of the audience on a fairly consistent basis. In a larger group, to give the impression that all listeners are being addressed individually, pick five or six individuals in different parts of the hall and pan from one to another at a leisurely rate. The most important audience member is the one directly in front of you. Personally address this listener each time you present a main point to give the audience the impression that you are creating a bond and sharing an important proposition.

Facial Expression

The key to effective facial expression is comfort and relaxation. Your facial expression tells the audience more about you than any other physical display. Practise before a mirror to learn to overcome the common problems associated with facial expression. A contrived expression usually results in a false, insincere look. Don't force it. Simply concentrate on the content of your speech. With experience, your expression will accurately mirror the levity or gravity of your subject matter.

Content

Purpose

Without a clearly defined purpose, your audience will remain unsure of the intent and direction of the speech. You should convey the purpose of your speech in your introduction. Generally, it can be condensed to one sentence or **thesis statement** that concisely states your intention. This affords the listener a focus and creates expectations that the effective speaker will meet during the course of the presentation.

Clarity

There are a number of ways of establishing clarity in the purpose of your speech and maintaining it throughout. Make sure your vocabulary is comprehensible to all listeners. If jargon is unavoidable, use it sparingly, and be sure to explain it fully. Whenever possible, illustrate difficult concepts with examples to promote understanding. Avoid too many lengthy sentences, which serve to disorient even the best listener. Finally, avoid digressions at all costs; once a presentation meanders, unity and relevance are sacrificed.

Development

The progression of your speech should be logical and well-organized. The pattern of the presentation should be determined in its purpose, and you should follow it through the duration of your speech. Present your points in a sustained manner, without long pauses. In most instances, you should incorporate a rising action to maintain audience interest, much as you would find in a good short story. If the pattern of presentation of your speech is complicated, use visual aids to help the audience follow your progression.

Transitions

Transitional devices--words and phrases, such as "consequently," "as a result of," "furthermore," "conversely," "in addition to," and "in conclusion," or even sentences linking one main point to the next, will contribute to the clarity and development of your presentation by indicating to the audience when one part of your speech has ended and the next has begun. Transitions also smooth your delivery, making your speech sound less disjointed.

Segmentation

Your presentation should have three clearly defined segments: introduction, body, and conclusion. The introduction should take up about 10 percent of the overall presentation time, and essentially should inform the audience of your objectives and create listener expectations for the balance of the speech. No detailed information should be given at this point. Rather, your introduction should make the audience aware of the focus and parameters of your presentation in a concise, non-threatening manner.

The body contains the gist of the speech. It should present ideas, information, or arguments logically and systematically. Because this is the lengthiest portion of your speech, you must be careful to properly pace the presentation of detailed information or concepts. Allow the audience adequate time to digest your material.

The conclusion, like the introduction, should be relatively brief and comprise about 10 percent of the presentation time. Use this segment to review the main points you presented in the body and allow the listeners a second opportunity to comprehend anything they may have missed or misunderstood. No new information should be introduced in the conclusion.

Visual Aids

Visual aids, such as boardwork, overhead transparencies, or slides, should be used to simplify the material presented orally. Plan to have each visual aid serve only one specific purpose--to better explain one important concept or idea. Your visual aids should enhance your presentation without overwhelming the audience. Show them long enough to satisfy note-takers, but when you move on to a different subject area, remove visuals to avoid confusion. Most importantly, visuals must be relevant to what's presented.

Ability to Answer Questions

An effective speech will generate audience interest--and questions. Audience members will pose questions to you either for clarification or for more detailed information. Address any questions at the conclusion of your presentation; answering them during the speech can result in disruptive digressions. When providing a brief answer, you should address the questioner and maintain visual contact. When giving a longer response, first establish a rapport with the questioner, and then direct your remarks to the audience in general. The question period is the last opportunity for you to clear up any confusion and to provide follow-up information; it is, therefore, a very important element of the presentation.

General Effectiveness

In addition to the individual elements mentioned above, adjudicators will consider a number of other questions when they are evaluating the general effectiveness of your presentation: Were the speaker's goals achieved? Was the material presented in a relaxed, professional manner? Could the speech be easily heard and understood? Was the available time used efficiently? Was the general impression created by the presenter a positive one?

Small Group Evaluation

Evaluating your group presentation is a different and somewhat complex task for the adjudicator, who must rate all the presenters in the group to arrive at an equitable group mark. In addition to the factors taken into account for the individual performances, a number of specific factors must be considered during the **symposium** and **parliamentary presentations**.

Introduction

Introduction of Topic

The **Chair** of a symposium and the Moderator of a debate should clearly and succinctly introduce the subject to be discussed or debated. The audience will derive more from the presentation if the subject is given a historical perspective or placed within an understandable context. If the subject is topical, reference should be made to the latest information available from the media. Long-standing topics of interest or debate should be introduced as items meriting continued interest. The Chair or Moderator must present this and other segments of the symposium or debate in a thoroughly objective manner. Subjective statements in the presentation should come only from the presenters.

Introduction of Presenters

In a symposium or debate, the Chair or Moderator should provide the audience with the name of each participant along with a brief biographical sketch. This might include the participant's academic and honourary degrees, affiliations relevant to the presentation, and current job title. All this must be done without bias toward or against the presenter.

The order of introduction in a symposium is relatively unimportant. The Chair usually starts at one side of the table and works toward the other. In a debate, the Moderator first introduces the individual or team supporting the issue or resolution under debate and then the individual or team against the resolution. The Chair of a parliamentary presentation will, for the benefit of the audience (members at large), introduce each member of the assembly in descending order of importance (Chair, Secretary, Treasurer, chairs of committees).

Introduction of Positions

Presenters of symposia do not so much present a position as a point of view distinctive from other presenters; that unique angle on the subject will be mentioned by the Chair in the introductory remarks. The Moderator of a debate will indicate the debater's point of view by the order of introduction ("for" versus "against" the resolution) and in any pertinent remarks during the introduction. Members of a parliamentary presentation will, as mentioned, be introduced by the Chair, who will announce their functions or positions.

Delivery

The evaluation criteria for group vocal and physical delivery remain the same as those in the individual presentations. The vocal categories are projection, pitch, articulation, pronunciation, and timing; the physical categories are posture, movement, gesture, visual contact, and facial expression. Because of space and especially time constraints, the evaluator only notes exceptional performances--good and bad--on the adjudication form in order to better determine the group's mark.

Group Dynamics

Control by Leader

The success of a symposium, debate, or parliamentary presentation often hinges on the knowledge and skills of the Chair or Moderator. The leader of any group oral exposition is responsible for the smooth and efficient presentation of ideas and information. Presenters, debaters, and meeting members tend to be more effective under the watchful eye and guidance of a skilled leader.

The symposium leader should have a working knowledge of the topic or issue at hand to better expedite the proceedings. Each speaker should be allotted an equal opportunity to present findings or explore issues. The moderator of a debate must maintain control during particularly heated moments and ensure that each debater doesn't exceed the agreed-upon time for presentation, retort, and closing remarks. The Chair of a meeting employing parliamentary procedure should maintain control without appearing overbearing or dictatorial. A thorough knowledge of the rules governing parliamentary procedure along with judicious guidance of the assembly will result in a smooth, effective meeting.

Division of Labour

Each member of a group presentation should contribute to the process and end result. Presenters of debates and symposia who fail to adequately address the issue do a disservice to themselves and their points of view. The audience needs a balanced presentation to form an educated opinion and fairly determine the merits of each point of view.

The group leader will decide on the time members are allotted for their presentations; what the speakers do with that time determines their level of success. While parliamentary presentations are somewhat less balanced in terms of division of labour, each group member should utilize the available time efficiently to contribute to the meeting's success.

Interaction

Since the majority of group presentations result in a single mark for the group, a group presentation should be considered a team effort. (The only notable exception is the debate.) One of the deciding factors in determining the success of a group is the "chemistry" or interaction among the members. Although compliance or consensus on every point raised is certainly not necessary, members of symposia and parliamentary presentations must show a willingness and ability to work as part of the group to solve problems. Adjudicators note the individual's skills both as a listener and as a respondent, and look for rapport among group members.

Transitions

Group presentations are susceptible to uneven and disjointed shifts from one idea or segment to the next. The combining of different personalities, thought processes, and speaking styles can often result in a presentation that lacks unity and flow. Whether as a leader or a presenter, you must make a special effort to follow a logical and consistent delivery. You can best do this by relating your material to the previous speaker's remarks. The use of transitional devices also helps other group members and the audience to follow the proceedings. This is especially important when the audience is comparing and contrasting different speakers' views in symposia and debates, and when group members are attempting to resolve a particularly complex issue in a parliamentary presentation. Chairs and Moderators should consider supplying brief summaries of individual presentations periodically to effect a better understanding of the subject.

Accomplishment

The group oral is a task-oriented process that is ultimately judged by what and how much is accomplished in a set period of time. In order to fairly consider the whole, the adjudicator must first determine the effectiveness of the individual parts. Did the Chair or Moderator provide insight into the subject without monopolizing presentation time? Did the individual presenters succinctly express their thoughts and findings in their effort to reach a common goal? Was there a satisfactory resolution to the issue? Was the meeting time constructively spent? Finally, did the group as a whole accomplish what it originally set out to do?

Visual Aids

The use of visual aids during a group presentation can present a number of logistical problems. Because stage space is more limited due to the extra tables or desks and chairs, not only is the placement of audiovisual equipment more problematic, but reaching it from the podium or lectern can also be awkward. The stage should therefore be arranged to facilitate easy use of the aids available, and any aids that will not be used should be cleared from the stage.

The proper demonstration of visual material is quite often time-consuming. If the majority of presenters use visual aids, less time can be spent on oral explanations, so visual aids should not be used unless they will significantly further comprehension of the oral material.

A related problem is information overload. If visuals are to be a part of the presentation, they should be simple and complementary, as too many visuals will confuse even the most attentive audience.

Ability to Answer Questions

Speakers in a parliamentary forum must be prepared to answer questions directed to them by other members. The windows of opportunity for such interchanges are specifically laid out in the rules governing parliamentary procedure. Answers should be directed to the questioners and the Chair. Any information at hand, such as prepared notes or statistics, can then be used to offer clarification.

Symposium presenters and debaters must be prepared for audience participation. Question and answer periods, usually scheduled for after the formal presentations, offer audience members the chance to explore specific points raised by the speakers. In such instances, the Chair or Moderator will acknowledge questions from the audience and direct each one to the appropriate speaker. Responses should be made directly to the individual questioners and be as concise as possible. Research and a solid knowledge of the material presented is the most effective preparation for answering questions.

Content

The adjudicator must appraise the content of the presentation in a number of ways. Traditionally, the content of a parliamentary meeting has been considered to be predominantly factual, with personal views presented only during discussion periods. The symposium is somewhat more subjective. The presenter provides research intermixed with opinion, so when evaluating the presenter, adjudicators listen for a balance of fact and opinion and try to distinguish the subjective from the objective material. The debate is difficult to evaluate for content. It is assessed as a skillful reworking of facts to fit the debater's position rather than as an attempt to objectively inform the audience.

General Effectiveness

When evaluating the general effectiveness of a group presentation, the adjudicator considers the contributions of the individual presenters and then designates a mark for the group. The adjudicator considers the following questions: Were the objectives of the presentation met? Did the group leader maintain control and direction? Did the presenters interact well with each other? Did each person contribute positively to the presentation?

SPEAKING FOR SUCCESS
THE CANADIAN STUDENT'S GUIDE TO PRESENTATIONS

INDIVIDUAL ADJUDICATION FORM

*Topic:*_____

*Presenter:*_____

DELIVERY (VOCAL)

Projection _____

Pitch _____

Articulation _____

Pronunciation_____

Timing_____

DELIVERY (PHYSICAL)

Posture _____

Movement _____

Gesture_____

Visual Contact _____

Facial Expression _____

CONTENT

Purpose _____

Clarity _____

Development _____

Transitions _____

Segmentation _____

Visual Aids

Ability to Answer Questions

General Effectiveness

*Time:*_____

*Adjudicator:*_____

$$\overline{100}$$

SPEAKING FOR SUCCESS
THE CANADIAN STUDENT'S GUIDE TO PRESENTATIONS

GROUP ADJUDICATION FORM

*Topic:*_____

*Presenters:*_____ *(Leader)*

_____

_____

_____

_____

_____

INTRODUCTION

of Topic _____

of Presenters_____

of Positions_____

DELIVERY

Vocal_____

Physical_____

GROUP DYNAMICS

Control by Leader _____

Division of Labour _____

Interaction _____

Transitions _____

Accomplishment _____

Visual Aids

Ability to Answer Questions

Content

General Effectiveness

*Time:*_____

*Adjudicator:*_____

$\overline{100}$

CHAPTER 5

The Informative Speech

- Types of Informative Speech
- Preparing the Informative Presentation
- Creating the Informative Outline
- Delivering the Informative Presentation

There are two main types of public speeches to choose between: the informative speech and the persuasive speech. Both types share a basic structure, with an introduction, a body, and a conclusion. Both require extensive planning, research, and editing. But there the similarities end.

In brief, an informative speech is objective. It offers factual material and supporting evidence. A persuasive speech, on the other hand, is usually subjective, incorporating a mixture of fact and opinion to present a particular point of view. Because the aims of these speeches differ significantly, the approach to research, construction, and delivery also differs.

So it's important to look at each type of speech separately and in some detail. This chapter concentrates on the informative speech.

When you are called upon to talk about what you *know*, rather than what you *think*, you will be expected to make an informative speech. The aim will be to transfer information from you, the **encoder**, to the listeners, or **decoders**, as expeditiously as possible.

Your listeners will likely have specific expectations about your speech, just as you will probably be able to make certain assumptions about them. The audience will want to learn more on a subject about which it already has an interest and probably some knowledge; it will be positively disposed toward, or at least neutral about, the subject matter. The informative speech, then, is chiefly concerned with satisfying the audience's curiosity. At the very least, your speech should provide information that is new, easily understood, and useful, and instructions on how it can be applied. If these expectations are unmet, the audience will feel unfulfilled.

Factual information should always be presented in an orderly, easy to follow fashion. Informative speeches are **deductive**; they lead audiences to reasoned conclusions by moving from general laws to specific examples. This funneling of information from the general to the specific allows listeners to follow the presentation of fact and evidence in a logical manner and arrive at valid conclusions.

The Structural Framework

The informative speech follows a structural framework not unlike that of a written essay. It has an introduction, a body, and a conclusion. A logical progression leads listeners to the same conclusion as that of the presenter and indicates *how* that conclusion was reached.

Four Varieties of Informative Speech

There are four varieties of informative speech: **instructional, presentational, descriptive**, and **explanatory**. Each variety has a specific application, predicated upon both the subject matter and the purpose of the presentation. Whichever of the four types of informative speech you choose, and whatever your topic, audiences will expect the presentation to be unbiased and evenly balanced. They also expect to be able to apply the material learned, so it must be relevant and useful.

The instructional speech

The instructional speech presents a pure process. It is essentially a "how to" speech. When preparing this type of speech, give careful consideration to ordering the steps presented so that listeners can clearly understand the process involved. Topics such as "How to Change a Tire," "How to Set a VCR Clock," and "How to Study" fall into the instructional category.

The presentational speech

The presentational speech usually involves reporting collected data and other research-related information. Present your findings in a logical, often chronological, pattern to enable the audience to comprehend the direction of your presentation and the relationship between the elements involved. Topics such as "The Effects of Acid Rain on Crop Yields," "Trends Between Boat Traffic and Manatee Mortality," and "A Survey of Canadian College Student Reading Levels" illustrate this presentational process.

The descriptive speech

The descriptive speech challenges you to maintain objectivity. Because point of view, vocabulary, and bias all play significant roles in the way things are described, you must strive especially hard to maintain impartiality in the presentation. Whether describing a place, a person, or an idea, your exposition must be clear and detailed, incorporating an evident organizational structure. "Skydiving--My First Jump," "Paris--City of Lights," and "A Day in a Television Newsroom" are typical descriptive speech topics.

The explanatory speech

The most detailed of the informative speeches is the explanatory speech, which presents background information and in-depth clarification. The subject must be introduced at a level that can be understood by all in the audience; your explanation must appeal to listeners' interest and be capable of being applied. If the speech is pitched at too technical or too simplistic a level, a sizeable portion of the audience can become alienated. The speech should offer its materials on a challenging level to avoid boring the more knowledgeable members of the audience. Descriptions should be interspersed with summaries to provide periodic reviews of information for those listeners unfamiliar with the subject matter. Sample explanatory speech topics include "Causes of World War I," "The Canada-U.S. Free Trade Agreement," and "The Trend Toward World Disarmament."

Constructing the Informative Speech

Although the approaches to informative speeches and their applications do vary, all four types are constructed in much the same way. Use the following general guide when you are creating an informative speech:

Preparation

When preparing the material for your informative speech, think about satisfying two basic criteria: the material should be useful and up-to-date. It should provide listeners with information they can readily apply in their day-to-day or professional tasks. This means you must choose the topic carefully and you must research it thoroughly in order to produce an effective informative speech.

Topic Selection

As with any speech, the selection of an informative speech topic should be made with the audience in mind. Does the audience have a shared interest in the proposed topic? Does each member of the audience have the same level of understanding of the subject? Can the information presented be applied, either personally or professionally?

Consider the topic's scope. Because available time is a limiting factor of any speech, you must be able to cover the topic you select comfortably in the available time frame. Don't make the mistake of attempting to present too general a subject or you won't be able to cover the subject matter adequately. Stick with a topic that is of a manageable breadth.

Since audience comprehension is greatly enhanced by visual aids, especially in the informative speech, consider the varieties and effectiveness of the visual aids available. Your audience will benefit most from seeing the actual objects that you are describing. If your speech is "How to Set a VCR Clock," then a VCR beside the podium would be an essential visual aid for a small audience. A large audience might benefit more from an overhead transparency that is easier to see from a distance. Whatever you choose, the visual aid should complement your presentation without drawing too much attention away from the speech itself.

Research

At every opportunity, try to incorporate relevant research and data in your informative presentation. There are two basic kinds of research: **primary research** and **secondary research**. Information generated by your own surveys and experiences is primary research. It is previously unavailable and exists only because of your efforts. Secondary research is information that has already been compiled and printed or taped by other persons. Libraries are traditional sources for secondary research; newspapers and magazines often provide the most current printed information.

The informative speeches that require the most in-depth research are the presentational and explanatory speeches. The presentational speech is based on existing research materials, and involves the orderly and methodical presentation of data that you have compiled. Your primary concern when making a presentational speech is the effective organization of these data. Guard against making assumptions about what the audience knows about the research procedure and results. If you overestimate the audience's knowledge of the subject, you might gloss over or even exclude key points and leave your listeners with insufficient information.

The explanatory speech also requires comprehensive research, but relies even more heavily upon your talent for **synthesis** and **analysis**. Synthesis refers to your ability to distil or synthesize general patterns or trends drawn from a range of sources. Analysis is the dissection, evaluation, and explanation of those patterns or trends. While the research component is important, the audience expects you to provide generalizations and analyses. Your task is to explain a theory, process, or event in a systematic and comprehensible fashion.

The research for the descriptive speech often relies upon first-hand experience. In your speech, you may draw on your memory to describe a person, place, or event in the first person. Whenever possible, supplement this information with up-to-date information from other sources, including library books and journals. Although primary and follow-up research is important, the balance of your preparation time should be devoted to effective word choice. Much of the success of a speech depends on the choice of language, which should be colourful and vivid.

Personal experiences or interests may also be drawn on for an instructional speech. The topic will likely be a familiar one, so the research will involve assembling interesting background information to provide a historical perspective or an illuminating context.

Construction

Once you've chosen your informative topic and compiled your research, you are ready to begin writing the speech. The construction of a speech is a process that involves a number of rewrites (or drafts). Each rewrite brings you closer to your final draft.

Prewriting

The **prewriting** stage can save a lot of time and effort during the construction of the speech. Before you begin to write, spend some time focusing on the major elements of the speech. Work toward preparing a skeletal outline of your speech.

The first prewriting step is **transcription**. List the information you have collected and the ideas generated by this research. Make a complete list without worrying about the order or value of the information, then leave the list for a day or two. This pause will equip you with increased objectivity for the next stage.

The second step of the process is evaluation. Review the list of facts and related ideas for pertinence, repetition, and redundancy, and strike out any tangential or marginally related points. The remaining points should relate directly to the speech. You must be ruthless in your appraisal of the relatedness of the elements in the list. Minor digressions at this stage can turn into major detours during the writing phase.

The third step of the prewriting process is editing. Modify any unclear or extraneous wording to provide a more streamlined, minimal outline that you can develop later. Avoid using descriptive words (adjectives and adverbs) at this juncture and concentrate on factual words and phrases. You will flesh out your speech with descriptions later in the process.

The final prewriting step is organization. Since the order of presentation is crucial to the informative speech, the points that remain after your editing must be logically organized. Each main point represents a full paragraph in the final draft of the presentation. Reposition the facts and ideas so that they flow logically from one point to the next. Once the information is logically ordered, you are ready to begin to write the speech.

Writing

The writing phase should be little more than the fleshing out of the skeletal outline you created during prewriting. Most writers construct three drafts of a speech, each one bringing the presenter closer to the finished product.

The first draft (sometimes referred to as the rough draft) is an extension of the organization stage of prewriting. Rough out a tentative introduction, body, and conclusion. It need be little more than a point-form version of the final speech. Position your main ideas logically and unite them with supporting ideas and evidence. Don't be concerned with stylistic and mechanical elements--these will be addressed later in the process.

When the first draft is complete, review the positioning of the supporting ideas in relation to the main points. Are they logically placed? Do they clearly support or illustrate the main ideas?

Most of your revisions will occur during the second draft. Your primary task here is editing the speech for content. Scrutinize the first draft carefully to check whether further additions and deletions are required. The need for changes will become increasingly apparent to you as your speech takes shape. Two important tasks will be performed during this rewrite: you'll review the speech for organization and logic for the final time, and you'll rewrite it in full sentence form with the proper use of grammar and punctuation. With a complete sentence and paragraph draft of your speech, you can easily check for structure, inconsistencies, and timing.

Now to the final draft of the speech. First, read aloud your second draft at a comfortable pace to determine how much time it will require for its presentation. If the speech is overly long, make further deletions. If it's not long enough, add further examples and supporting evidence.

When you are satisfied with the completed speech, transcribe the complete sentence and paragraph draft in point form onto note cards. This will help to reinforce your main points and their order in your mind. And because only the main points are copied, the note cards promote an extemporaneous presentation--polished, concise, and flexible.

Delivering the Informative Speech

Now you've prepared your informative speech, you should consider how to deliver it. The delivery will reflect the nature of the speech itself. The informative speech is expository, so the explanations in your speech should be impartial. Maintain your objectivity throughout the preparation and delivery of your presentation so your speech will be truly informative.

Guidelines for Informative Presentations

The listener or reader of a speech inevitably carries certain cultural expectations about the message. Whether it is written or presented orally, we have been taught to expect three major divisions in the message--a distinct introduction, body, and conclusion. Because they are expected and they serve a distinct purpose, each of these three elements must be present in your informative speech.

Introduction

The introduction should offer your listeners a clear statement of intent. Alternately referred to as the **thesis statement** or topic sentence, this statement should concisely outline the purpose and goals of your presentation.

Observe the following guidelines when you are presenting the introduction to your informative speech:

1. *Prepare the audience for the presentation.* Your introduction should create listener expectations by introducing the subject and outlining your goals. If the subject is particularly challenging or difficult, provide background information.

2. *Create interest in the subject.* Appeal to your listeners' sense of curiosity and interest by indicating how they can benefit by paying close attention to your presentation. Take advantage of the fact that people tend to be more attentive when they expect to receive something of value.

3. *Initiate objectivity in the introduction.* Informative presentations must present information in a balanced, unbiased fashion. Establish this objectivity in your introduction.

4. *Introduce the topic in general terms.* Informative speeches are by nature deductive. Begin your introduction with a general reference and lead to a more specific discussion in the body.

5. *Keep the introduction brief.* If you disclose too much during your introduction, your speech may end up being boring and redundant. A concise introduction will set up the balance of the speech without prematurely revealing the major points and supporting evidence.

Body

Present the bulk of the information, supporting evidence, and examples in the body of your speech. Arrange the information logically and deductively, encouraging listeners to follow your reasoning and to better realize how you arrived at your conclusions. You'll want to devote about 80 percent of the total time of your speech to the body. Because it is the largest segment of your presentation, the information must be attractively packaged and presented to maintain audience interest.

Consider the following suggestions during your presentation of the body of the speech:

1. *Organize and present the material logically.* Audiences learn most effectively if material is presented to them in a logical order. Present historical information chronologically; structural and hierarchical material is usually presented from top to bottom.

2. *Present the main idea first, followed by the supporting evidence, details, and examples.* You should discuss and illustrate each main point or idea before you present a subsequent or consequent point. Dealing with one point at a time enhances audience comprehension.

3. *Differentiate between fact and opinion.* You can offer opinions in your informative presentation provided you clearly identify them as opinions, and not facts.

4. *Use transitional devices.* Because you are presenting a large amount of information, make a point of using clear transitional devices. These transitions prepare listeners for shifts in topic focus.

5. *Use visual aids to explain difficult concepts.* Not only do visual aids enhance audience understanding of challenging material, but they also recapture audience interest. Use simple visuals, strategically placed in the body, to increase audience comprehension and attention.

6. *Summarize difficult material and related ideas regularly.* If the body of your informative presentation is especially long and challenging, periodic summaries or reviews will help your listeners better understand the process or content.

Conclusion

The final segment of the informative speech--the conclusion--summarizes the body and highlights the major points raised. Audiences pay particular attention to the conclusion; it is their last opportunity to acquire any of the main points they may have missed initially.

Keep your conclusion relatively brief. Like the introduction, it should consume about 10 percent of the total presentation time. Exploit the fact that audience attention levels are higher at the end of a speech. If you provide a concise review of your presentation in the conclusion, you'll keep your listeners' attention during this critical stage.

Keep in mind the following guidelines when presenting the conclusion:

1. *Signal the start of the conclusion.* Audiences require a vocal prompt to recognize the transition from body to conclusion. Listeners automatically pay greatest attention to the concluding segment of a presentation.

2. *Review only the main points of the presentation.* Conclusions must be brief to maintain audience attention. Review only the main points to conserve time and provide a digestible review.

3. *Maintain the same order of presentation in the body and the conclusion.* Audiences will remember the information more easily if you present it to them twice--in the same order.

4. *Don't introduce new information in the conclusion.* The introduction of new information in the conclusion can only confuse an audience that simply expects a review of your previously stated material. If you feel the information is important enough to be included in the presentation, you should place it in the body of the speech.

5. *Draw parallels and indicate trends when summarizing the presentation.*
    Audiences expect you to synthesize and analyze your presentation. This
    summing up process should culminate in a series of general statements
    that encapsulate the main points of the speech.

Answering Audience Questions

The question and answer period is a useful segment of the informative presentation. It gives you the opportunity to clarify portions of your presentation and
to further explore areas of specific interest to listeners. It can also be a time
for a cordial interchange of questions and ideas between you and your listeners,
and can result in the audience's gaining a deeper understanding of the subject.

Follow these guidelines when conducting the question and answer period:

1. *Announce the question and answer period at the beginning of the speech.*
    Questions posed during the speech can be distracting for you and for
    members of the audience. Avoid this by informing the audience that
    time will be provided for questions at the conclusion of your presenta-
    tion.

2. *Do not evaluate questions.* Treat all questions, even poor ones, fairly.
    Avoid inadvertently passing judgment on question quality with state-
    ments such as "That's an excellent question." Such an observation im-
    plies that prior questions were of a lesser quality.

3. *Answer questions pleasantly and politely.* By treating listeners and their
    questions fairly and politely, you maintain poise and respect. A polite
    response to an impolite question is an effective way to secure audience
    approval.

4. *Use paralanguage when responding to questions.* The voice and the
    body are effective tools for maintaining a rapport with your listeners.
    Paralanguage can improve the quality of any response.

5. *Look at the audience when answering a question.* Maintain eye contact
    with the questioner while the question is asked. This will indicate your
    interest in the question. When you are answering the question, look at
    the entire audience to convey the importance of your response.

6. *Admit to not knowing all the answers.* Such an admission could criti-
    cally affect audience response in a persuasive presentation, but the in-
    formative audience is much more patient and forgiving. If you don't

know the answer to a question, either request help from the audience or offer to research the answer.

7.   *Keep responses to questions brief.* This is especially important when a number of listeners have questions or when a time limit has been imposed. If there are remaining questions, you might offer to meet with interested parties afterward to answer them.

Sample Informative Outlines

Study the following sample outlines to get a better idea of how to plan and construct an informative speech.

A Descriptive Speech

The first outline deals with an influential nineteenth-century civil rights leader named Sojourner Truth. Although a predominantly descriptive speech, it also incorporates elements of the presentational and explanatory speeches to broaden its appeal.

Objectives

The speaker sets her objectives before embarking on the construction of the outline. The objectives she identifies include the purpose of the speech, the thesis statement or topic sentence, and the main ideas to be conveyed in the presentation.

SOJOURNER TRUTH

Objectives

Purpose
To inform the audience of the accomplishments and influences of Sojourner Truth.

Thesis Statement
Sojourner Truth's experience as a female slave, her deeply rooted faith, and her natural eloquence made her a worthy and indomitable champion of abolition, women's rights, and religious freedom.

Main Ideas

I.Despite her lack of education and considerable language barriers, Sojourner became an articulate and influential rhetorician.

II.The adversity she experienced provided the impetus for her advocacy of the disadvantaged.

III.The issues Sojourner grappled with remain timely ones; the messages she provided bear close examination, even a century after her death.

Outline

After establishing the objectives, the speaker constructed the outline, using the three divisions of the speech--introduction, body, and conclusion--as the primary building blocks. By compartmentalizing the speech, she was better able to manage its development and direction.

OUTLINE

Introduction

I.   "God is everlasting. There was no beginning till sin came. All that have a beginning will have an end. Truth burns up error." (Katz)

II.   Mystery surrounds Sojourner one hundred years after death.

      A.   Remarkable and inspirational story bears retelling.

III. *Sojourner Truth's experience as a female slave, her deeply rooted faith, and her natural eloquence made her a worthy and indomitable champion of abolition, women's rights, and religious freedom.* (thesis statement)

IV.   Acquaint ourselves with the person and the legacy.

Body

I.   Her crusades were responses to personal experience.

      A.   Childhood.

          1.   One of about a dozen children born on a Dutch estate in New York in 1797.

2. Parents and master died. At age of nine, sold for $100 in slave auction to plantation owner.

B. Adulthood.

1. Language problems; she spoke only Dutch and her new master spoke only English.

2. Severe whippings given her by master.

3. She married and bore five children, all of whom were sold illegally.

II. Religion signalled turning point in her life.

A. Offered an escape from the pain she experienced.

B. Provided a calling.

1. "Sojourner" implied travel.

2. "Truth" implied spreading the word of God.

III. Oratory became her life's work.

A. Causes supported.

1. Became an evangelist in 1843; toured Massachusetts.

2. Argued for abolition in 1850; toured western New York and Midwest.

3. Delivered most famous speech in 1851 at Women's Rights convention in Akron, Ohio.

4. Included economic assistance for freed slaves as one of her causes after Civil War.

B. Rhetorical devices.

1. Presence.

2. Metaphors.

3. Personal experience.

4. "Low (familiar) style."

5. Humour.

Conclusion

I.   Sojourner's Legacy.

    A.   Influence continued after her death in 1883.

        1.   Causes she championed (religious freedom, civil rights, women's rights) owe much to her efforts.

        2. Example she set paved way for other minority leaders.

II.   "The wondrous experiences of that most remarkable woman would make a library, if not indeed a literature, could they all be gathered and spread before the world." (Pillsbury)

An Instructional Speech

The next example is an outline for an instructional speech. Because it describes a process, this outline showcases the step-by-step chronological system of organization and presentation. "How to skim read" is a topic with a fairly narrow scope. Its audience is probably academic or professional. Consequently, this presentation doesn't require the devices used in the previous outline to broaden its appeal. Like the previous outline, though, it does follow a series of steps to ensure consistency and understanding.

HOW TO SKIM READ

Objectives

Purpose
To instruct listeners on how to extract the greatest amount of information from printed material in the least amount of time.

Thesis Statement
Skim reading, properly performed, yields about 70 percent of the information in a deductive chapter or article but requires only 30 percent of the time usually expended to read the entire piece.

Main Ideas
I.   Deductive writing is usually prefaced by an introduction designed to inform the reader what to expect and a conclusion designed to review the main points raised.

II. The main idea in a deductive paragraph is invariably found in the first or second sentence.

III. Nouns and verbs supply most of the meaning in a sentence.

IV. Accelerated reading rates increase both reader attention and retention.

Outline
The outline based on the above objectives is chronological. The speaker has carefully ordered the steps to facilitate listener comprehension. Note that the introduction creates listener expectations by outlining the speaker's goals. Only vital information is presented in the body to spare listeners from having to remember non-essential material. The conclusion is a succinct review of the main points found in the body. This streamlined approach is typical of an instructional or process speech.

OUTLINE

Introduction
I.   Two types of accelerated reading.

     A. Scan reading.

         1. Reading for specific information.

         2. Approximate idea where information to be found.

     B. Skim reading.

         1. Reading for general impression.

         2. Initial reading or a review of previously read material.

II. Skim reading particularly useful when great volume of material must be digested in little time.

III. *Skim reading, properly performed, yields about 70 percent of the information in a deductive chapter or article but requires only 30 percent of the time usually expended to read the entire piece.* (thesis statement)

IV. Textbook chapter a good application of skim reading.

Body
I. Prereading.

  A. Bibliographic information.

    1. Book title.

    2. Chapter title.

    3. Author's or editor's name.

    4. Place of publication.

    5. Year of publication.

    6. Edition.

  B. Graphic material.

    1. Figures.

    2. Appendices.

II. Skimming.

  A. Read first two paragraphs completely.

    1. Chapter preview presented at beginning.

    2. Key words and phrases identified.

  B. Read first two sentences of each subsequent paragraph.

    1. Main ideas stated at paragraph beginnings.

C. Skim balance of each paragraph for nouns and verbs.

    1. Nouns and verbs convey most of meaning.

D. Read last two paragraphs completely.

    1. Chapter synopsis and conclusion presented at end.

    2. Key concepts reviewed.

III. Supplemental reading.

A. Chapter summary.

B. Review questions.

Conclusion
I. Skim reading has three major components.

A. Prereading.

B. Skimming.

C. Supplemental reading.

II. Only first two and last two paragraphs should be read completely.

III. Skimming an effective way to quickly read or review a chapter.

CHAPTER 6

The Persuasive Speech

- Motivating the Audience
- Preparing the Persuasive Presentation
- Creating the Persuasive Outline
- Delivering the Persuasive Presentation

You have been asked to make a speech that will revolve around your ideas and opinions about a specific topic. A persuasive speech will be required. You should assume that your listeners won't necessarily agree with you; at best they will be neutral, at worst hostile. They will probably only be willing to accept information that corroborates their own point of view, yet, in spite of their interest in your topic, they likely have incomplete knowledge or a biased view of it. These assumptions will likely put you on the defensive.

The persuasive speaker has a significantly more difficult task than the informative speaker. The content and delivery of your speech become as important as the preparation of the speech, and in addition to presenting ideas and opinions in a convincing and palatable form, you must first establish credibility with a critical audience. Much of your success will hinge upon gaining and keeping the audience's confidence. Listeners must feel they can trust you before they will be willing to listen to and accept your ideas and opinions.

There are a number of factors to consider when trying to build up credibility on stage.

1.   *Respect.* Try to display respect for the audience. Listeners will react positively and respect your opinions if you give their opinions serious consideration--even if they differ from yours. This mutual respect is essential in building a rapport with the audience.

2.   *Credentials.* Our society places a high value on certification as proof of legitimacy. Not only do degrees, diplomas, and certificates signify credibility, but the experience gained provides a comforting practical basis for trust.

3.   *Sincerity.* Insincerity is usually equated with dishonesty. Always be sincere. Even if this means you must dispute beliefs held by some listeners, the audience will regard you as honest and trustworthy.

4.   *Poise.* If you can cope tactfully with adversity during a presentation, you will command the respect of the listeners. By remaining confident and poised, you project certainty and faith in the proposition.

Target Audiences

Don't expect to be able to win over every member in the audience. Even partial success in a persuasive speech can be considered a victory. Your audience will comprise three types of listeners: those who support your proposition; those who are either receptive or indifferent to your proposition; those who are opposed to your proposition. It is unlikely that you will be able to persuade those who strongly disagree with your position to shift their position. They are probably too set in their beliefs to listen objectively and change their minds, especially on the basis of a single speech.

You should concentrate on the other two listener types. Your secondary target is those listeners who already agree with the proposition. Try to further consolidate their support with your speech. But your main focus, your primary target audience, will be listeners who are receptive to your proposition but who are uncommitted to either side of the issue. You can achieve the greatest impact by winning over this usually sizeable segment of the audience.

How to Persuade?

In a sense, the persuasive speech is the most psychological of all oral presentations. It depends upon your talents to accurately "read" the audience, determine the level of support, and offer ideas and supporting evidence reasonably and effectively. Listeners will only accept a point of view at variance with their own if they are convinced, not coerced, into acceptance. No one reacts favourably to being pressured. The audience should *want* to accept your position by the presentation's end.

You can use either deductive or **inductive** reasoning as your governing approach when making informative and persuasive speeches, but the greatest success is usually derived from an inductive approach. Put simply, you should persuade the audience to accept your credentials and reputation as they relate to the topic, to fully understand the issue, to agree with the arguments advanced, and to act upon the recommendations.

Five Steps to Persuasion

Your goal is to reduce listener barriers to acceptance and increase the probability of persuading undecided listeners to accept your proposition. Try following these five motivational steps:

1. *Get the audience's attention.* The attention stage serves to inform the audience of the topic and of the speaker's sentiments. Employ an arresting method of getting the audience to think about your topic as quickly as possible--right from the introduction. Typical attention-get-

ting devices are the **rhetorical question** and the startling statement. Both methods, used skillfully, will engage listeners in the issue.

2. *Demonstrate the audience's need to know.* Listeners pay particular attention to persuasive presentations when they feel they can benefit from the information. It is up to you to convince listeners that the ideas in your speech impact directly on their lives. By suggesting to the audience that the ideas have value, you further strengthen its desire to know.

3. *Satisfy the audience's need to know.* Once you have convinced your listeners of the importance of the issue, they require proof that your position is the best one. Clearly and convincingly state your belief or suggested action within the context of the issue. Don't hesitate to supply facts, figures, and examples; they play a pivotal role in winning the audience over.

4. *Visualize the results.* The vision or image of what the speaker proposes is a powerful persuasive tool. Ask the audience to visualize the situation that would result after your proposals are adopted and you reinforce their faith in your ideas. Not only do your recommendations appear more plausible or tangible when visualized, but they are more apt to be acted upon.

5. *Request the audience's action.* This final motivational step represents the goal of every persuasive speaker. Your request for action must be a reasonable one; however, overly ambitious or radical proposals do little but scare off supporters. Listeners are more likely to comply with a call for action if they sense the urgency of the situation. Because listeners either forget to act or regain their complacency when given an indefinite time to act, don't forget to impose a time frame for their response.

Approaches to Persuasive Presentations

There are different approaches to making a persuasive presentation. In the popular low-key approach, you progress through the five motivational steps and allow time for the appeals to take effect. The majority of effective salespeople use this approach. Slowly and systematically they reduce customer suspicion or skepticism, and often the result is a sale.

If the situation calls for a more active inducement to action, the argumentative speech may be more appropriate. It focuses upon the presentation of a series of emotional appeals, often at the expense of logic. While the argumentative approach has been a successful one for a variety of motivational speakers (most notably television evangelists), its application is limited.

Constructing the Persuasive Speech

The persuasive speech is constructed in much the same way as an informative speech. The following steps are a general guide for the construction of a persuasive presentation using the motivational sequence:

Preparation

When preparing a persuasive speech, you must build a strong case for your point of view and recommendations. Thorough research plays a pivotal role in the success of your presentation. Without hearing a solid battery of supporting evidence, the audience will remain leery and unconvinced of the proposition's merits.

Although the informative speech often succeeds on the basis of good research alone, the persuasive speech must be presented convincingly to succeed. The subjectivity of your speech will make it one-sided. While preparing it, however, remain aware of both sides of the issue. Periodically compare the strengths of your points against those of the contrary position and you will assemble a more convincing argument.

Topic Selection

Persuasive speech topics have two clearly defined sides, referred to as the "pro" and "con" positions. You must choose one side and support it from start to finish. To encourage a favourable audience reaction, try to choose a subject that is topical and affects the listeners directly. Avoid popular persuasive speech subjects such as "Capital Punishment" and "Euthanasia." Though basically sound choices, they don't have personal significance for many people and are best presented in a **debate** or symposium format, where they would receive more thorough treatment.

How much do you know about your potential audience and their concerns? It's important to consider them when selecting a topic and point of view. It is unlikely that an assembly of retirees will have a great interest in current educational issues or that a gathering of travel agents will show much enthusiasm for a persuasive presentation on medical ethics. A good persuasive topic appeals to specific audience interests and is reasonable in its scope.

Once a topic is selected, it must be worded in the form of a clear and concise proposition, whose function is similar to that of the thesis statement in the informative speech: it states the subject and the speaker's point of view.

You must thoroughly understand your proposition and analyze it for a workable strategy before you begin to research for evidence to support your point of view. Knowing which kind of proposition you want to make will help you figure out how to write your speech. The three general categories are fact, value, and policy. When you make a proposition of fact, you must then prove or disprove an alleged or perceived fact. You will state your proposition in the positive or the negative. Your speech will be designed to persuade listeners to accept specific supporting facts and, ultimately, the proposition itself. Here are some examples of propositions of fact:

- Diet plans do not result in permanent weight loss for the vast majority of people.

- The three party system is the most effective political system.

- John F. Kennedy was killed by a lone gunman.

When you make a proposition of value, you make a judgment or evaluation on an issue. Your speech must provide justifications for the belief that something is good or bad, right or wrong, justified or unjustified. You will present specific evidence in support of the proposition. These are examples of propositions of value:

- Animals are effective subjects for the testing of cosmetics.

- Television creates negative role models for children.

- Sports stars are not worth the salaries they command.

When you make a proposition of policy, you are making a statement about creating a policy or effecting a change in an existing policy or course of action. This proposition concerns future action and always contains the word *should*. The following examples are propositions of policy:

- The Free Trade Agreement should be rejected.

- Air bags should be standard equipment on all new road vehicles.

- AIDS research should receive greater government funding.

Research

How can you persuade your listeners that your argument is sound? Any persuasive presentation relies upon its supporting evidence to convince listeners of its merits. Without substantiating evidence, you'll have little hope of establishing credibility.

Like the informative speech, the persuasive speech should incorporate research from a number of sources. Although both primary and secondary research can be included in the presentation, secondary research (information compiled by persons other than the presenter) carries greater weight because of its perceived objectivity. But even secondary research in a persuasive argument is open to suspicion. As both the persuader and the compiler of the research, you are obviously biased, and the audience will look for signs that you have chosen to present only that evidence that supports your contention.

There are a variety of ways to counter this suspicion. By using information written by recognizable and respected authorities, you draw a parallel between your ideas and those of experts. Using different sources gives the impression that the research is wide-ranging and compiled without prejudice.

Construction

The persuasive speech and the informative speech employ the same basic framework, incorporating the introduction, body, and conclusion as their primary divisions. However, the elements of a persuasive speech follow a somewhat more inductive order, and unlike the informative speech, which fully discloses its intentions in the introduction, the persuasive speech sets out to pique the listener's interest and then gradually discloses the speaker's intent.

Prewriting

The prewriting of the persuasive speech is rather more complex than for any of the informative presentations, since, in addition to providing information, you must also choose and apply persuasive techniques. As a result, your focus during prewriting must center on the audience. In order to decide whether to include a particular idea or piece of supporting evidence, ask yourself, will it strengthen the audience's belief in the proposition? Effective audience analysis will lighten your task. If you can tailor your message for a specific group of receivers, you can better control listener response to your message.

When preparing a persuasive speech, you'll want to construct an outline similar to the one described in the previous chapter. The skeletal outline provides the basis for the final draft of your presentation. List in point form the information and ideas generated by your research. This first step, transcription, furnishes you with a working draft. Tabulate the facts and ideas without thinking too much about whether or not they'll remain in the final draft.

In the second step, evaluation, you must judge your material for relatedness and also for persuasive potential. Drop from the list any items not germane to the argument. Eliminate any ideas difficult to support or defend. If you include weak or indefensible material beyond this stage, your presentation's success can be severely threatened.

Editing is the next prewriting step. The remaining facts, ideas, and opinions should be further streamlined to facilitate the actual writing. Alter awkward and repetitive wording, and eliminate descriptive words for the time being.

Finally, organization. Reorder the points you want to use in your speech. Since most persuasive speeches present their appeals inductively, you may wish to begin by presenting your more specific points and then move to the more general ones.

How can you make the final decision about which research to include in your speech? Research for persuasive speeches requires a comprehensive appraisal. When you evaluate your research, look at the following properties:

1. *Fact.* Factual content is the cornerstone of any persuasive presentation. It provides irrefutable information on which to base the argument.

2. *Interpretation.* Information that can be made to conform to a specific point of view has a high interpretive value. Statistics are often used as evidence because of their versatility: they can be adapted to support almost any contention.

3. *Persuasion.* Listeners respond to one or a combination of appeals. Appeals on the basis of social, biological, and psychological needs and desires determine the persuasive potential of the research.

Writing

Expect to create three drafts of your persuasive speech. The first draft (or rough draft) is a point-form expansion of your outline. Position the ideas and supporting evidence within the framework of the introduction, body, and conclusion so that they conform to the chosen pattern, whether deductive or inductive.

Make any major revisions during your writing of the second draft. This draft should be written in complete sentence and paragraph form so that you can proofread the speech and accurately time its length.

The final draft is the completed, note-card version of your speech. It should contain only your main theses, properly ordered to present your ideas and evidence in the most convincing fashion. This point-form version will help you speak freely, without being tied to rigidly reading your speech.

Delivering the Persuasive Speech

From your very first few sentences, an audience can tell what kind of speech you are presenting. If a thesis statement or topic sentence emerges early in the introduction to inform listeners of the speech's purpose and to create expectations about what will be discussed, they know to expect an informative speech. Much of the impact of a persuasive speech is generated by its unpredictability.

There are strategies and tactics you can use to keep your audience listening. First, try to keep the element of surprise on your side. It is crucial to maintaining the audience's interest, which means that it's a good idea not to start off your presentation by announcing your topic sentence. Just as a sales presentation won't work if a sales pitch is presented too soon, so a persuasive speech won't be effective if the topic sentence is presented too soon. First you must convince your listeners of a need before you can expect them to react positively. Instead of revealing what your proposition is, begin your speech by succinctly describing the problem in your proposition. This strategy, based on the specific to general organization pattern common to inductive presentations, compels listeners to infer the extent of the problem and formulate possible solutions. It also lets you present your points without being prejudged.

Guidelines for Persuasive Presentations

Every type of speech should be constructed around three major divisions--the introduction, body, and conclusion. The functions of these divisions, however, will vary depending what kind of speech you are writing.

Introduction

The initial segment of the persuasive speech has two important functions: to grab the audience's attention, and to initiate one or a series of appeals. Observe the following guidelines when you are presenting your persuasive introduction:

1. *Capture the audience's attention.* Listeners are usually unsure of what to expect from a persuasive speech, so what you say initially and how you say it will make a distinct impression. If your speech is on a contentious issue, introduce it insistently, even argumentatively, such as with a startling statement--this will set the mood for the balance of the presentation. If your speech is more persuasive than argumentative, it will need a softer opening, such as a reference to the subject or a rhetorical question.

2. *Create interest in the subject.* After getting the audience's attention, you must quickly create and sustain its interest in the subject. Interest is most effectively generated by showing a need or creating a desire for something.

3. *Introduce the topic in specific terms.* By employing the inductive approach, you immediately confront your listeners with evidence that supports your proposition. Specific supportive examples will reduce audience resistance to different ideas and opinions.

4. *Indicate your position on the issue.* The introduction must clearly inform the audience of the issue and your position or sentiment, pro or con.

Body

The body of your persuasive speech should concentrate on further developing the listeners' need for a resolution to the problem and then satisfying that need by offering a solution. Consider the following suggestions when preparing the body of your speech:

1. *Position the strongest persuasive points where they will be most noticed.*
    Listeners are most likely to notice and remember points placed at the
    beginning and end of a list. Begin an argument and end it with the
    strongest points that support it.

2. *Focus on one side of the issue.* Persuasive presentations are by nature
    subjective. Don't try to give a fair and equitable coverage of the pro
    and con sides. This will only reduce the strength of your argument.
    Refer to the opposing position as little as possible.

3. *Support ideas and opinions with facts.* Opinions and ideas are more
    readily accepted if they have been prefaced by convincing factual
    evidence. Provide your listeners with substantial factual evidence to
    make them more receptive to your ideas.

4. *Use persuasive wording.* While the ideas presented are important in
    any persuasive presentation, the way you word them is also important.
    Vocabulary and **syntax**, properly employed, are effective persuasive
    tools.

5. *Use transitional devices.* When ideas interrelate, they are better under-
    stood and remembered. Transitional devices help listeners understand
    the relatedness of ideas and signal shifts in topic focus.

6. *Use visual aids to illustrate important ideas.* Visual aids have a high
    impact when used sparingly, so reserve their use for the most important
    points in your presentation. Placing them strategically heightens
    audience attention at crucial points of your speech.

Conclusion

The most important part of the persuasive speech is the concluding segment.
You don't need to review the major points of your speech in the conclusion;
that function was performed when you asked the audience to visualize the results
near the end of the body of the speech. The sole purpose of the conclusion is
to get listeners to respond to your request for action or approval. Your persuasive speech is only successful if your listeners are moved to respond
favourably.

To make your conclusion persuasive, like a salesperson closing a sale, you
must be both patient and convincing to the end. Here are some guidelines to
consider:

1. *Don't introduce new information in the conclusion.* Any additional sup-
    porting evidence after the visualization stage will only confuse listeners.
    The audience should be emotionally willing to consider the request for
    action without the need for further evidence.

2. *Base the request for action or approval only on the evidence presented.*
    Listeners will respond to what they've heard and not necessarily to what
    was implied. Limit the request to the points discussed in the speech.

3. *Be reasonable in the request.* Overly ambitious requests for action are
    never acted upon. Propose a course of action that is workable.

4. *Keep the request brief.* Listeners can only remain motivated for so long.
    If the request for action or approval is a prolonged one, the impact and
    immediacy of the proposition will quickly wane.

Answering Audience Questions

Questions directed at persuasive speakers are generally more challenging than
those posed to informative presenters. The question and answer segment of a
persuasive presentation encompasses facts, opinions, points of view, and sometimes even personalities. Despite the potential for losing some hard fought
ground, most presenters perform commendably when responding to audience
questions. Speakers confident in their research and position on the issue can
answer questions with ease and comfort. There are a number of guidelines
governing the question and answer period:

1. *Announce the question and answer period in the introduction.* To dis-
    courage listeners from interrupting the presentation with questions, in-
    form the audience that questions will be dealt with at the end of the
    speech. Not only will the audience refrain from interrupting the speaker,
    but many of its questions will be answered as the speech progresses.

2. *Never ask a persuasive speech audience for comments.* Speakers who
    request comments put themselves at risk. By having to respond to a
    negative comment, the speaker is placed on the defensive--not the ideal
    position for a persuader. Limit the audience's feedback to questions
    pertaining to the presentation.

3. *Field questions pleasantly and politely.* An effective way of diffusing
    listener anger or displeasure is by answering questions politely. By
    engaging questioners courteously, the speaker maintains poise and
    respect.

4. *Use paralanguage when responding to questions.* Paralanguage is an effective tool for maintaining a rapport with the audience. By using the voice and the body to provide secondary messages, the speaker can exercise control over the audience and the situation.

5. *Maintain visual contact with the audience.* Look at the questioner while the question is being posed, and then expand the visual field to include the entire audience when providing the answer. This indicates interest in the question and underscores the importance of the response.

6. *Uphold the correctness of the position presented.* Always refer to the proposition in positive terms and avoid reference to the contrary point of view. If the opposing point of view must be mentioned, refer to it in neutral language.

7. *Keep responses to questions brief.* If a number of listeners have questions, try to answer as many as possible by limiting the length of the responses. In the event that a time limit has been imposed, offer to answer any remaining questions afterward.

Sample Persuasive Outlines

The following two sample outlines show the planning and construction of persuasive speeches. While the persuasive speech outline shares a number of features with the informative outline, the objectives and methodologies differ significantly.

The first example outlines a speech on the importance of recycling. The speaker has chosen to base her presentation on a proposition of policy; it deals with a recommended course of action for the future and incorporates the word *should* in the proposition. Note that the objectives differ from those employed in the informative speech; both speeches have distinct purposes, but the thesis statement has been replaced by a proposition. The main ideas have been replaced by one central and a number of supporting arguments.

RECYCLE!

OBJECTIVES

Purpose
To motivate the audience to save the environment by recycling materials.

Proposition
Consumers *should* use the recycling facilities available to preserve the environment.

Central Argument
Common varieties of trash can easily be recycled.

Supporting Arguments
I.   Recycling consumes little personal time.

II.   Recycling facilities are easily found.

III. Recycling can have an enormous positive impact upon the environment.

Outline

The objectives provide the basis for the persuasive outline. Like the informative outline, this one uses the three divisions of the speech--introduction, body, and conclusion--as a guideline. The outline follows the inductive format, leading with supporting evidence and culminating with a general statement. This example clearly shows a need and then satisfies that need as the speech progresses.

Introduction
I.   North Americans engage in the systematic and indiscriminate destruction of their environment.

    A.   Typical person will generate 600 times his or her adult weight in garbage in a lifetime.

    B.   A 150 pound adult will create 90,000 pounds of trash in a lifetime.

Body
I.   The current situation.

    A.   Four types of recyclables.

        1. Aluminum.

        2. Paper.

        3. Plastic.

        4. Glass.

  B. Pollution generated by production.

        1. Air pollution.

        2. Acid rain (sulphur dioxides).

        3. Water pollution.

  C. Pollution generated by disposal.

        1. Air pollution (incineration).

        2. Water pollution (contamination of water table).

        3. Landfills.

II. Remedies.

  A. Precycling.

        1. Buy bulk products.

        2. Buy products in recycled packaging.

        3. Buy products in recyclable packaging.

  B. Recycle aluminum.

        1. Reduces production energy consumption by 95 percent.

        2. Reduces air pollution (sulfur dioxide emissions cut by 95 percent).

        3. Reduces amount of landfill.

  C. Recycle paper.

1. Paper constitutes 40-50 percent of disposed waste.

2. 62 million newspapers purchased each day of which 44 million are thrown away.

3. 44 million newspapers equivalent to 500,000 trees.

D. Recycle plastic.

1. 50 varieties of plastic on market.

2. Plastic containers now number coded for easy recycling.

E. Recycle glass.

1. Glass constitutes 8 percent of municipal garbage.

2. It never wears out; can be recycled forever.

3. Coded by colour for easy recycling.

Conclusion
I.   Recycling is successful.

A. Already landfill need reduced by 34 percent.

II.   Visualize a cleaner environment.

III. Request audience action.

A. Not enough has been done; we're still at risk.

B. More recycling is required to save environment.

C. Success depends upon each individual.

The next example is an outline employing a proposition of fact. It states an opinion as if it were a fact and proceeds to support it with convincing evidence. Because it deals with a perceived fact, this outline relies upon irrefutable facts as arguments in support of the proposition.

THE POLITICAL GAMES

OBJECTIVES

Purpose
To convince listeners that the Olympic Games should be modified or discontinued.

Proposition
The Olympic Games have evolved from a sporting to a political event.

Central Argument
The Olympics are remembered more for their political headlines than for their athletic milestones.

Supporting Arguments
I.   Nations, not athletes, compete against each other.

II.   Political idealogies compete in the guise of athletics.

III. Professional athletes, commercial endorsements, and drug controversies have made a mockery of the Olympic spirit.

Outline

The outline incorporates the central and supporting arguments of the objectives in a logical, inductive pattern. Because the Olympic Games are held every four years, the arguments are presented chronologically.

Introduction
I.   The original intent of the modern Olympics.

   A. To provide an opportunity for the young of all nations to meet and better understand each other through athletic competition.

   B. To promote world peace, understanding, and harmony.

Body
I.   Nationalism and the Olympics.

A.   The Olympics promote flag-waving and patriotism.

1. The Games are only awarded to nations willing to spend millions of dollars on facilities.

2. Many host nations have large homeless and starving populations.

B. The Games encourage stereotyping of nations and races.

1. Certain nations expected to excel in specific sports.

2. Certain races expected to excel in specific events.

3. Rich nations expected to succeed because of coaching and facilities.

II. Political ideologies and the Olympics.

A. The Games as a political platform.

1. 1936 Munich Games showcased Nazi ideology and the Aryan ideal.

2. 1968 Mexico City Games provided a racial platform for some Black American athletes.

3. 1972 Munich Games marred by politically motivated murder of some Israeli athletes.

4. 1980 Moscow Games boycotted by many Western nations in response to war in Afghanistan.

5. 1984 Los Angeles Games boycotted by Eastern Bloc nations in retaliation for 1980 boycott.

6. Long-standing ban against South Africa for its racial policies.

7. Sanctions against New Zealand for competing against South Africa.

III. The loss of innocence and idealism.

A. The use of professional athletes.

1. Soviet Union's use of alleged amateurs in hockey competition.

2. The U.S.A.'s all-pro Olympic basketball team in the 1992 Barcelona Games.

B. The politics of money.

1. The widespread use of amateur athletes to endorse commercial products.

2. The skirting of regulations governing payment to amateurs by deferring payment for commercials.

C. Controlled substance abuse.

1. The use of steroids to enhance performance.

2. Inadequate testing for substance abuse.

Conclusion

I.   The Olympic Games have lost their focus

A. Athletic events now a sideshow to political showcases.

II. Visualize the Olympic Games without politics.

III. The Olympics should be reexamined for worth.

A. Two options exist.

1. Restructure the Games to recapture their spirit and intent.

2. Discontinue the Games.

Chapter 7

The Small Group Presentation

- Types of Small Group Presentations
- Small Group Presentation Personnel
- Preparing the Presentation
- Delivering the Small Group Presentation

It is likely that you will find yourself speaking as part of a small group one day. Privately or publicly, small groups perform much of the work in business and society. In a small group presentation, participants and listeners can exchange ideas as part of the educational and problem-solving processes. This format provides more latitude and a wider range of views than an individual presentation. It is also less constraining than a large group situation; everyone in the group has the opportunity to contribute to the meeting.

Speaking in a small group adds a new dimension to public speaking. All participants will need to cooperate to an extent, whether in agreement or disagreement with one another. Audiences tend to experience a "warm up" period with a speaker--that is, they spend the first minute or two of a speech familiarizing themselves with the speaker's rate of speech, syntax, pronunciation, and delivery style. When there are several speakers, audiences must work all the harder to comprehend what's being presented.

Planning, then, is a crucial element in the successful small group presentation. Because any group tends to benefit from leadership, the first task of your small group should be to select a group leader or **Moderator**. In essence, the group leader is a facilitator, serving not only as coordinator of the various presenters, but also as intermediary between the group and the audience. It is the Moderator's responsibility to serve as "gatekeeper," regulating the presentation time of each speaker and overseeing interaction with the audience. By encouraging audience participation and promoting goodwill between presenters and listeners, the Moderator can positively influence audience perception of the presentation. Qualities to look for when choosing the person to lead your group are good organization skills, a sense of fair play, and the respect of the group. Ideally, a group leader is familiar, though not necessarily in agreement, with the various points of view the members hold on a given subject.

There will be marked differences between your individual presentation and your group effort. Group presentations are somewhat reactive in nature. This means you can no longer be simply a speaker--you must now be an adept listener as well. Much of what you say will depend upon the content of other members' presentations. You'll be a more effective and interesting small group speaker if you listen and refer to the discussion on stage and not just your prepared notes.

You'll also need to employ both strategy and tactics when participating in a group presentation. Your strategy will be the comprehensive presentation plan prepared by the group. This will anticipate the direction of the presentation and offer a loosely structured plan for action. When the discussion deviates from this anticipated plan, your group must resort to tactics. Tactics are effective reactive changes in the strategy, used either to maintain an individual's or group's stated position or to counter an opposing argument. With practice, you'll find that logic and quick thinking are the most effective elements in a tactical situation.

This chapter introduces the three most popular forms of small group public presentation. Each method has evolved into a specialized format that is conducive to a specific type of topic exploration. The format is chosen on the basis of the objectives of the presentation and determines how the subject will be presented to the assembly.

Symposium

If you are called upon to deliver a relatively brief presentation along with several others on a common topic, theme, or issue, you are part of a symposium. The symposium, often part of a larger event (the conference), usually includes speaker interaction after the formal opening speeches. During the final phase of the assembly, the audience is given the opportunity to ask questions. The symposium's presentations are usually educational, and are designed to enlighten the audience, not only about the subject matter, but also about how the speakers arrived at their conclusions.

While there is no set number of presenters, the symposium usually features three to six speakers. Typically, there are four presenters, presided over by a Moderator. Because this series of presentations is a cooperative effort, the Moderator rarely has to deal with disputes or personality issues. The leader's primary duty is that of time manager, ensuring that all presenters and questioners have sufficient opportunity to speak.

The typical symposium is partitioned into three segments: one-third of the time is scheduled for speaker presentations, one-third for speaker interaction, and one-third for audience questions. Most symposia last two to three hours-- and since a great deal of information is exchanged, it's two to three hours of hard work for both presenter and listener. Conference goers, then, can realistically expect to attend a maximum of two symposia each day.

Objectives

Since, as a symposium speaker, you will already be familiar with your colleagues' research and points of view, your objective should be to instruct and inform the audience. And because the symposium is an educational exercise, every effort must be made to enhance audience comprehension.

The primary objective of the group is to present as complete an overview of the subject as possible. The scope of the presentation rests, of course, on the number of presenters; the more presenters, the more complete the coverage. In instances where an extensive topic is to be covered by few presenters, each speaker can cover two phases to broaden the scope.

The secondary objective is to shed new light on an issue. This is effectively achieved by promoting audience interest and interaction with the speakers. However, the speakers can't do it all alone; the audience plays an important role in the success of a symposium. Audience questions during the last stage of the symposium can uncover further information of interest. Tailor your presentation to encourage audience questions.

Preparation

Concerted preparation should ensure that the content of your presentation does not overlap with that of another presenter, and should seek to eliminate other pitfalls. In advance of the symposium date, the Moderator will schedule a series of meetings with contributors. The first meeting should be devoted to determining the parameters of the presentation and the division of labour among group members. Once the topic, issue, or theme has been agreed upon, each presenter should volunteer to cover a certain phase or portion of the subject matter, contingent upon his or her area of expertise. The Moderator will prescribe the limits of coverage to ensure there is no overlap.

In most instances, each scheduled speaker has ten minutes to speak but if this is not the case, there must be consensus on the length of presentations. To be fair, all presentations should be of the same length. The Moderator, in consultation with the group, will determine the order of presenters, based on the logical sequence of elements.

As a group, you will then want to discuss the various research sources available and the paths you intend to take in the coverage of your particular areas.

Such preplanning guards against duplication and guarantees consistency of approach.

At your second meeting, be prepared to present the Moderator with your biography, the historical perspective of your subject, and an outline of your presentation. This information enables the Moderator to prepare introductions to each speaker and the subject. Group members should discuss their outlines to further establish the focus of the symposium. Any inconsistencies, duplications, or tangents should be remedied before preparation continues.

Subsequent meetings can address new research and its effect on the presentation as a whole. In addition, you may wish to discuss the probable direction of your group discussion and possible questions from the assembly. Such preparation can anticipate potential problems and provide your group with a working strategy.

Personnel

The symposium is a highly interactive meeting that ultimately includes not only the presenters on stage, but the audience as well. As the meeting progresses, it becomes less formal, and this greater informality encourages wider participation, but the personnel involved in the symposium still have specific roles to play.

Moderator

The Moderator, who must orchestrate the meeting without being overbearing, plays an important but delicate role in the success of the symposium. The Moderator's duties are:

> 1. to chair the preparatory meetings and offer suggestions and guidance to the presenters.
>
> 2. to introduce the topic and the presenters at the symposium.
>
> 3. to oversee the group discussion and ensure that it remains relevant.
>
> 4. to offer periodic explanation, analysis, and summary of the discussion.

5. to encourage audience participation during the forum and to recognize members of the audience.

6. to provide a summary of the main points of the discussion.

7. to adjourn the symposium.

Presenter

The symposium revolves around the speakers' presentations. As a presenter, you are in a unique position. You are a member of a team, yet you offer information and research independent of that of other members. You must not only be knowledgeable and articulate, but also a quick and flexible thinker. As a presenter, your duties are:

1. to convene at the request of the Moderator and supply the group with rough and final drafts of your presentation.

2. to offer constructive criticism of other presentation drafts.

3. to clearly and concisely present the final presentation draft to the assembly.

4. to engage in topical conversation with other presenters.

5. to succinctly answer any questions posed by the audience.

Process

Once the audience has assembled, you and the other members of the symposium take your places on stage. The presenters and the Moderator should have easy-to-read name cards on the tables to facilitate audience questioning.

Symposia can be either formal or informal presentations. The level of formality is usually determined by the type of audience present and the nature of the subject. If you find yourself in a formal situation, you'll stand at the podium during your formal presentation. If the atmosphere is more relaxed, only the Moderator will stand during the speaker introductions. You can either stand at your desk or remain seated.

After getting the audience's attention, the Moderator begins proceedings by clearly stating the topic of discussion and the agenda--that is, the program specifying the length of the presentations, the group discussion, and the question and answer period. Audiences are more attentive when they know what to expect during a presentation.

The Moderator then introduces the presenters in their scheduled order. Each introduction should include the speaker's name, position, qualifications, and relevant biographical notes. A perspective and stance on the subject should also be included in the introductory remarks. These introductions are an important element of the symposium, since audiences tend to be more positively disposed to speakers they know something about.

The Moderator next announces the first speaker. The Moderator times the presentation and rises briefly two minutes before the allotted time has elapsed, giving the speaker warning to proceed to his or her conclusion or closing remarks. If the presenter is still speaking after the allotted time has run out, the Moderator again rises and remains standing. This procedure is repeated until all the presenters have spoken.

Once the formal presentations are concluded, the Moderator announces that the speakers will engage in a dialogue. This presents an opportunity for the presenters to question one another, but it also gives the audience a better understanding of the interrelationships and variances in your points of view. This flexible, informal section of the symposium often involves a lively interchange of ideas and perspectives on the subject. During this time, the presenters may defend their statements, modify their positions, or react to prior remarks.

The Moderator times the discussion and oversees the conversation but ideally, offers little guidance. However, if the discussion digresses, it is the Moderator's responsibility to bring it back on track. If the discussion has stalled, the Moderator should prompt the presenters by restating, summarizing, or pointing out relationships between the points of view. If an argument develops, the Moderator must tactfully intervene and resume the program.

When the time allotted for the group discussion has expired, the Moderator announces the start of the **forum**, or question and answer period, and invites questions from the audience. The Moderator must recognize the questioner before he or she can speak. It is the Moderator's responsibility to ensure that the questions are clearly understood by the presenters. If the questions are inaudible or obscure, the Moderator restates them for the benefit of presenters and audience alike. If the subject matter is difficult or if the discussion is hard to follow, the Moderator should periodically recap the discussion to enhance comprehension.

When the available time has been exhausted, or if there are no further questions, the Moderator summarizes the symposium. This summary should include highlights from the individual presentations, the group discussion, and the forum. The Moderator then thanks the presenters and declares the symposium adjourned.

Sample Symposium Topics

Symposium topics should be easily segmented into logical sub-categories. Here are some typical symposium subjects (the sub-categories are offered in the order they would be presented):

Literacy and the College Student

1. Methods of measuring literacy.

2. Literacy levels in the general population.

3. How literacy is currently developed.

4. Readability of college textbooks.

5. Methods of increasing student literacy.

The Canada-U.S.A. Free Trade Agreement

1. History of Canadian-American trade relations.

2. European Economic Community model.

3. Political factors influencing free trade.

4. Cultural factors influencing free trade.

5. Analysis of the agreement.

6. Impact of free trade.

Serial Murderers

1. Documented serial killings of the past century.

2. Ratio of male-to-female serial murderers.

3. Psychological profile of the serial murderer.

4. Social factors influencing serial killers.

5. Media treatment of serial murderers.

6. Treatment and punishment of serial killers.

Panel

If you are invited to speak on a topic in common with other participants--but you do not meet as a group beforehand to discuss the subject--you will be taking part in a **panel**.

The panel is similar in many ways to the symposium. Both small group formats engage experts in a discussion on a common topic. The major difference is in the level of cooperation. Symposium participants regularly consult one another before the assembly to ensure complete coverage; panel participants do not. The panel format requires its participants to discuss a subject without regard for totality of coverage.

There are other differences too. As a panelist, you must still carefully research and organize information for your presentation, but a fully prepared and presented brief is not expected. Think of a panel presentation as a supervised conversation among from four to six people in front of an audience. Because it is a conversation, it cannot be as intricately planned as a symposium presentation. The bulk of the conversation is a series of questions and unplanned responses, loosely based on preparatory notes made by the participants.

Like the symposium, the panel is instructional; it shows the audience that a number of experts on a given subject can hold widely disparate points of view. But the panel's spontaneity severely restricts its usefulness as an educational forum. Unlike symposium participants, who may only speak when given permission to do so by the Moderator, once the panelists have made their two-minute opening remarks, they may interrupt one another any time to make a point. This lack of structure impedes the audience's ability to take notes.

Properly performed, the panel is a unique experience for the audience. The panelists speak to one another in an informal, impromptu manner, while the audience "listens in" on the conversation and then has an opportunity to make critical comments.

Panel discussions can last from one to two hours, depending on the scope of the topic and the number of questions and comments from the audience. The Moderator can regulate the flow and direction of the presentation by controlling audience input and mediating when the discussion becomes too argumentative.

Objectives

As a speaker on a panel, your primary objective will be to demonstrate to the audience only one of a wide range of viewpoints on a single subject. Your presentation can be unstructured, requiring the audience to sift fact from personal bias.

Your secondary objective is to encourage audience input, as this increases awareness and concern for the topic under discussion. Successful panel discussions leave audiences better informed about specific issues and motivated to think or act in a specific manner.

Preparation

Panel discussions are often sponsored and organized by an interested group or agency. A committee will be formed to decide who should be invited to participate as a panelist and who should chair the panel. The selection of effective panelists is pivotal to the success of a panel presentation. Committee members know a successful panel discussion needs participants who will engage in lively, thought-provoking dialogue. They will probably draw up a list of experts on the topic to be discussed and look for those who are animated and have distinctively different or even controversial opinions on the topic.

The Moderator will be chosen as someone with a firm understanding of the subject as well as the skills to guide the proceedings; the Moderator will maintain an effective balance of panel conversation and audience input without being overbearing.

Once the panel is finalized, the Moderator will arrange a meeting of all the participants, or, if this is not possible, will inform each individually of the procedure to be followed. During these preliminary discussions, the Moderator will become acquainted with the various points of view. This will help in the framing of the introductions and allow the Moderator to better anticipate the direction of the panel discussion.

Personnel

Because the panel discussion requires a high degree of participant interaction, as a panelist you should simply relax and concentrate on your primary role--that of conversationalist. Be tactful and respectful of the other panelists. Any supervision or guidance should be left to the Moderator.

Moderator

As host of the discussion, the Moderator should take a relaxed attitude during the proceedings. Ideally, the Moderator will allow conversation to proceed without often needing to intervene or contribute to the discussion. The Moderator's duties are:

1. to interview panelists and brief them on their responsibilities and the procedure to be followed.

2. to introduce the topic and the panelists to the audience.

3. to explain the format of the panel discussion to the audience.

4. to exercise tact and discipline if the conversation becomes argumentative.

5. to ensure the discussion remains on topic.

6. to regulate audience participation by recognizing questions from the audience.

7. to serve both panelists and audience, providing periodic updates on the information presented.

8. to adjourn the panel.

Panelist

You are most valuable as a panelist when you concentrate on the subject matter and refrain from attacks and criticisms of the other participants. Your duties as a panelist are:

> 1. to meet with the Moderator and learn the procedure to be followed.

> 2. to fully prepare by researching and organizing the points to be presented.

> 3. to speak in a clear, loud voice for the benefit of the audience.

> 4. to politely answer or comment on audience questions and statements.

> 5. to freely share information and opinions with the assembly.

> 6. to accept the guidance of the Moderator in matters of direction and discipline.

Process

The panel discussion is about to begin. Once the audience has assembled, you, the other panelists, and the Moderator take your assigned places on stage. You should all have been supplied with name cards to facilitate dialogue with the audience. The Moderator stands, states the rules governing the presentation, and introduces the topic of discussion and the members of the panel. Each introduction should include the panelist's name, qualifications, and a summary of his or her position on the subject.

Rise briefly when your name is called to better help the audience identify you. For the balance of the presentation, you, the Moderator, and the other presenters will normally remain seated.

The Moderator then calls on each panelist in order (right to left, or left to right) to make a brief opening statement. Your opening statement should better acquaint the assembly with your position. Be sure to restrict yourself to the agreed-upon time.

After each speaker has made a statement, panel discussion begins.

Like the symposium, the panel encourages audience participation, but there is a difference. Rather than waiting for a more formal forum segment, the Moderator will recognize questions and comments from the audience *during* the panel discussion once the discussion is well under way. If the audience is allowed to contribute too soon, there is a danger that panelists will spend more time answering audience inquiries than presenting their pivotal points. The Moderator should forewarn the panelists before allowing audience questions. All conversation on stage should cease when an audience member has been recognized so that the question or comment can be heard and understood. Conversation should not resume until the question has been answered by the panelist to whom it was directed.

The Moderator should punctuate the discussion with analysis or explanation when the discussion becomes muddled or technical. Should the need for mediation arise, the Moderator will tactfully intervene and restore order before the conversation continues.

Prior to the close of the panel discussion, the Moderator may choose to offer a brief summary of the ideas presented. The contributors are then thanked and the meeting is adjourned.

Sample Panel Topics

Good subjects for panel discussion are topical issues that directly affect the audience, are controversial in nature, and inspire a passionate response from both presenters and listeners. Here are some sample panel topics accompanied by possible approaches or points of view:

Athletes and their Escalating Salaries

1. Athletes should have capped salaries.

2. Because their careers are brief, athletes should not be subject to salary restrictions.

3. No salary restrictions should apply in a free, capitalistic society.

4. Athletes who receive product endorsements should have their salaries capped.

5. Sports fans should not absorb salary increases in their ticket prices.

6. Teams, not individual athletes, should be subject to salary restrictions.

Television Violence and Children

1. Parents should assume all responsibility for their children's viewing habits.

2. Violence is a part of our society and should not be excluded from television programming.

3. All programs containing violent acts should be preceded by an on-screen warning.

4. Programs containing violent acts should not be aired before 10:00 PM.

5. Cartoons should be censored since they are directed toward children and are among the most violent television programs.

Health Care Funding

1. Health care is a right and should, therefore, be funded completely by the federal government.

2. Health care is a service whose cost should be the responsibility of the user.

3. Free health care should be provided only to those individuals who cannot afford it, including the unemployed and the retired.

4. Health care should be recognized as part of the free-enterprise system; health care practitioners should be allowed to freely advertise and set their own fees.

5. Employers and their employees should divide equally the cost of employee health care programs.

Debate

You've been asked to be one speaker on a team of two that will argue formally against another team of two on a pro and con issue. As a debater, you can expect plenty of tension between your team and the opposing team. Aside from the fact that both sides have agreed to disagree on an issue, there is little harmony and cooperation between the presenters. Because debates can become quite heated, they are carefully regulated by a Moderator.

Of all the small group presentations, the debate is the most contentious. If you think you'd enjoy a contest for audience approval and a battle of wits, the debate is for you. "Play to the audience" when on stage. You won't be able to persuade your opponents that your position is the right one, but, through logical reasoning and effective presentation, you might be able to convince the audience that your position is the stronger of the two.

Debates are unique in their presentation of conflicting arguments. In spite of the obvious disagreement between the opposing teams, the contest is held in a fair and civil manner. Strict rules govern the debate process, allowing each side the opportunity to present and counter arguments logically and methodically. You and other participants are given strict guidelines with respect to time, methodology, and convention. If you violate any of the rules, not only do you incur a reprimand from the Moderator, but you also stand to lose audience favour.

Objectives

When you participate in a debate, your objective is simple: to win. But who decides if you win? Traditionally, debates are evaluated by the Moderator, who also acts as the **judge**, or by a panel of judges. Political debates, especially since the development of the electronic media, are scored by the viewing audience and an impartial press. Judges attempt to remain objective in their awarding of points. A team that systematically and logically erodes the opposition's arguments will invariably earn the majority of points. Because judges are also susceptible to the influences of style, and our society places a value on wit, emotional appeal, and quick thinking, judges will be more impressed with a team that presents its arguments in an entertaining, humorous way.

Make your arguments entertaining, but keep the logical construction and presentation of an irrefutable argument uppermost in your mind. You can best attain this objective through painstaking planning, solid evidence, and flexibility during the presentation.

Preparation

Teammates may either work together as equals, or one of you may be declared the group leader. The leader would then ensure that all preparation was done on schedule and would rule on decisions if a stalemate occurred between group members.

You'll also have to make some initial decisions with your opposition. Although each team works independently in the preparation and presentation of its arguments, you must first agree upon the **proposition**, the statement on which the debate is based. The proposition should be worded as clearly as possible in the form of a **resolution** so both sides fully understand the **parameters** affecting the issue.

You'll probably want to get together with your teammate a number of times before the debate, but perhaps the most important meeting is the initial one. Use this time to analyze the proposition very carefully in order to clearly understand both positions on the issue. Any questions or comments about the proposition should be directed to the Moderator at this point.

The planning stage of a debate is extremely painstaking. Not only must your team construct its arguments, but you must try to fully anticipate the opposition's counter-arguments. In essence, your team will construct two arguments on the issue--yours and that of your opposition. This will help you strengthen your own case and reduce the probability of surprise from your opponents. Prepare a comprehensive strategy and your team should perform more effectively during the tactical part of the debate.

Timing is the primary consideration in the planning process. Debates are strictly timed to ensure both sides receive equal opportunity. What your team does with its allotted time determines the effectiveness of your presentation. You have to work hard for the entire scheduled debate, not just when you are speaking. The effective debater develops the ability to listen critically *and* keep extensive notes of the opposition's arguments and rebuttals. Good time management at and away from the podium is crucial.

Another major consideration is flexibility. Effective teams know that a strategy is simply a plan, and even good plans often go awry. Successful debaters help each other by sharing observations and ideas, and conferring while the other team presents its points. Combine solid preparation and a willingness and ability to change and you'll greatly reduce the chance of being upstaged in a debate.

Discuss your strengths and weaknesses freely with your partner when you plan your strategy and speaking order. Are you a strong opener who would do best delivering the initial presentation? Or would you be most effective in a reactive role after the debate has assumed a definite structure? Both roles are critical to success; there can be no weak links in a debating team.

The indispensable tool of any debating team is the **brief**--essentially your battle plan or strategy for the debate. Work on putting together a working brief for your team before you construct your individual presentations. Formulate it during the early planning stages as a guideline for further strategic development. Like most tentative plans, the brief will change its structure and focus as your planning develops. In its final form, the brief will outline your strategy by providing a projected plan of the opposition and your team's probable response.

The core of an effective brief is logic. All the points outlined in the brief must arise from, or relate back to, one central argument or issue. **Brainstorm** with your teammate during the early stages of brief preparation. Write down any and all ideas relating to the central issue; let them sit for a day or two, so you become more objective, and then edit and evaluate your points. Group those you want to keep according to their focus, and edit them further for repetition and redundancy. Place the points in their most logical and advantageous order. Now you can formulate your individual presentations with a target in mind.

If your team is supporting the pro, or affirmative, side of the proposition, you must assume the **burden of proof**. This means you must demonstrate that your proposition is superior to the **status quo** (or current system or situation). When constructing your individual presentations, you must not only demonstrate why the current system is weak, but also show how your proposals will remedy that system. This burden of proof requires comprehensive research and painstaking analysis.

If your team is supporting the con, or negative, side of the issue, you will be assuming the **burden of rebuttal**. Because the onus is on the pro side to prove that change is desirable, it is traditionally believed that the negative side is the easiest to win. Even if change is deemed desirable, the con side can rebut the measures proposed as insufficient, or worse than the status quo. Whichever side of the debate you are on, your team must familiarize itself with the strengths and weaknesses of both positions before you can construct your individual presentations.

Personnel

At all stages, and regardless of the speaking order, there should be an equal division of labour between team members. You will each share in the planning, research, and presentation.

Leader

Most debating teams appoint a leader to oversee presentation, preparation, and strategy. The leader usually speaks first, setting the stage for subsequent presentations. The duties of the leader are:

> 1. to interpret the proposition.
>
> 2. to organize the preparation, including the division of labour and research.
>
> 3. to help formulate a strategy based on an analysis of both pro and con positions.
>
> 4. to anticipate counter arguments by suggesting possible tactical approaches.
>
> 5. to present the opening speeches in both the constructive and rebuttal rounds.

Second

In a two-person debating team, the **second** is responsible for countering the opposition's initial arguments. The second should be prepared to modify the team strategy in light of the opposition's initial presentation. As the last speaker in the final (or rebuttal) round, you must supply a strong summary of your team's position. The second's duties are:

> 1. to help interpret and clarify the proposition.

2. to contribute to the research and planning of the team's presentations.

3. to help formulate the strategy and possible tactics to be employed during the presentations.

4. to present the closing speeches in both rounds of the debate.

Process

A formal debate consisting of an affirmative team, a negative team, and a Moderator is a classic confrontation presentation.

For the benefit of the audience, all the participants on stage should have cards on their tables indicating their names and their position on the proposition. If the winning side is to be determined by a panel of judges, and not the Moderator, the judges may be positioned either on stage or in the first audience row. The proposition, phrased as a resolution, should be prominently displayed in clear view of the audience.

The debate is brought to order by the Moderator, who states the resolution and the rules and times governing the debate. In some instances, the Moderator will provide a brief overview of the issue, citing its history and impact upon the assembly to better prepare the audience for the discussion. Each of the debaters is introduced and will rise as his or her name is called.

The debaters speak in a predetermined order to ensure fairness and order during the presentation. Your speech is carefully timed by the Moderator. When you have only one minute left before your time allotment has expired, the Moderator warns you by rising. At your allotted time, you'll be stopped abruptly by the Moderator.

A team debate takes exactly one hour of presentation time, with each debater having the opportunity to speak twice. The first round of presentations--the **constructive speeches**--establishes your position on the issue. Your speech during this round cannot exceed ten minutes. The second round--the **rebuttal speeches**--allows each side to respond to the other's arguments. Your speech in the rebuttal round cannot exceed five minutes.

Speaker order cannot be modified from the following pattern, for it guarantees an order equitable to both sides:

Constructive Speeches

First Affirmative

First Negative

Second Affirmative

Second Negative

Rebuttal Speeches

First Negative

First Affirmative

Second Negative

Second Affirmative

The Moderator initiates the debate, calling on each debater in turn to speak, and thanking each one before introducing the next. Traditionally, you'll get a brief recess after the last constructive speech so you can plan your tactics for the rebuttals. After a recess of no more than ten minutes, the Moderator reconvenes the debate by introducing the first negative speaker.

Apart from delivering the introductions and maintaining order during the debate, the Moderator does not contribute to the proceedings until the end of the rebuttal segment. After the final rebuttal speech, the Moderator thanks both teams for their presentations. If a panel of judges is present, it now has time to deliberate, with input from the Moderator, on the outcome of the debate. The Moderator then announces the panel's decision and usually provides reasons for the decision. If the Moderator is the sole official, he or she should announce the decision immediately after the last rebuttal speech, again providing reasons for the decision.

Sample Debate Resolutions

Debate propositions fall into three categories: fact, value, and policy. They are always phrased as resolutions. Here are some examples:

1. *Resolved*: That global warming threatens all plant and animal life. (fact)

2. *Resolved*: That capital punishment is a deterrent to murder. (value)

3. *Resolved*: That religion should be a component of elementary school curricula. (value)

4. *Resolved*: That all abortions should be outlawed. (value)

5. *Resolved*: That all males should have two years of mandatory military service. (policy)

6. *Resolved*: That all nations possessing nuclear weapons be required to disarm. (policy)

CHAPTER 8

The Formal Meeting

- Parliamentary Procedure
- Formal Meeting Personnel
- Meeting Documents
- Primary and Secondary Motions
- Meeting Management

If you asked every person attending a formal meeting what his or her expectations were for the meeting, you would probably receive as many answers as there were respondents. One person would prefer not to attend because he fears not having anything genuinely important to contribute. Another would be anxious that she might be upstaged by superiors or peers in a group situation. Only a small proportion of participants would say that they truly felt comfortable and positive about attending meetings.

Reluctant participants are not the only reason for group leaders to consider carefully whether or not to call a meeting. Sometimes meetings are called for no reason other than that the leaders think it is expected. They labour under the illusion that meetings will automatically produce the results they desire. In addition, meetings, especially in the business forum, aren't cost free; salaried participants put their other work on hold to meet for an hour, a day, or even a number of days.

When a great deal of time and money is at stake, stringent rules must be observed. Meetings will only be truly successful if there is a good reason to meet, if there is an **agenda** to follow, and if all the participants are prepared. Before you hold any formal meeting, consider the following three important questions:

Is this formal meeting really necessary?

Can the issue be resolved without a formal meeting--perhaps by informally contacting the people directly involved? If so, this would be a significantly more efficient way to proceed.

If you decide that a few of the key personnel must meet, keep the meeting small and informal, so that you won't be wasting the time of nonessential people. For example, if a firm's National Coordinator of Marketing and Sales is experiencing reduced sales in one sector, there is no immediate need to call a meeting with representatives of all geographic sectors. Only those personnel directly involved with that sales sector should meet initially. If there is no resolution or if more feedback and alternative ideas are required, then a general meeting should be called.

Is this agenda realistic?

There's nothing more frustrating than to attend a meeting with an endless list of issues on the agenda. Don't be too ambitious when setting an agenda. Remind yourself of the human factor--people can only deal efficiently with a finite number of issues before they lose their effectiveness. Determine the length of the meeting by establishing a set time period within which all the agenda items must fit. This usually results in a more streamlined, efficient meeting. Another method is to set the agenda and then allot an appropriate amount of time for each item.

Agenda items must be set with a specific purpose in mind, and the **Chairperson**, or Chair of the meeting should determine the relevance of each item to all meeting participants. If an item is of interest to only a few people in the meeting, it might be better if they met to address it later among themselves.

Are the participants prepared?

A key element in running an efficient meeting is the level of preparedness of the participants. Because proper preparation takes time, be sure those attending the meeting receive their agendas as early as possible. Traditionally, agenda items are submitted to the Chair at least four days before the scheduled meeting so that there is time for the Chair and the **Secretary** to put together the agenda and send it to participants. Participants will need a minimum of two or three days to research and prepare their briefs for the meeting.

While not every item on the agenda is of specific importance or interest to each member, participants should have some familiarity with all the items or issues on the agenda. Research by individuals can often be cursory in areas they deem to be of secondary importance, but even cursory research should enable them to contribute. In fact, quite often the most useful contributions at meetings are offered by third parties who possess an objectivity not always found in those primarily concerned.

Of course, if you are submitting an item for an agenda, you must be fully versed in the subject or issue. You will be expected to address the item and both inform and attempt to persuade the others of your views. So that you can respond well to questioning, take time to research both sides of the issue. Your presentation of an agenda item should be concise and professional. If the item is concerned with figures or trends, consider using visual aids to make the information easy to grasp. Efficient Chairs will set specific time frames for presentations and questions to expedite proceedings. Plan accordingly when constructing your presentation packages.

Meeting Limitations

A **meeting** can be defined as a gathering or assembly of persons for the purpose of discussing and/or resolving specific issues. However, meeting participants often achieve significantly less than they intend, usually because they experience one of a number of barriers to effective communication.

Awkward seating arrangements is one such barrier. The round-table seating plan served King Arthur admirably because his intention was to demonstrate the equality of all who met there. In modern meeting situations, however, the group leader usually sits at the head of the table, as this easily establishes the leader's primary role. The leader can best exercise control of the meeting when in an obvious position of authority and in clear view of all participants. Similarly, you should be able to clearly see all the other meeting participants. If you can see each speaker's facial expressions and body language, you'll be able to understand better what is being said.

The number of people present at a meeting can hamper good communication and positive group dynamics. The more people in attendance, the smaller each person's contribution. When eight or ten people meet, general participation and discussion is limited. Large meetings also tend to inhibit shy people from contributing to discussions.

The personalities of the individuals involved in a meeting can also play a large part in whether or not the meeting proceeds smoothly. Some people assume meetings must be adversarial because they involve debate. Disagreements are natural in the meeting forum, but participants should strive to remain objective in their problem solving and have a positive, cooperative attitude.

Parliamentary Procedure

Despite the many limitations to large group meetings, you can increase the chances of realizing success by learning more about the skills and techniques of group interaction. There is an established protocol for formal meetings that is designed to help participants overcome the barriers to communication found in the large group setting. If you use it properly, **Parliamentary Procedure** will help you conduct your meeting in an equitable and effective fashion.

The purpose of any meeting is to engage the group in a cooperative problem-solving discussion. Parliamentary Procedure, or **Robert's Rules of Order**, simplifies this process by imposing a framework of rules to govern the conduct of participants in a formal meeting. These guidelines streamline the discussion process, helping the group to achieve its goals effectively and efficiently.

Here are some of the guidelines for Parliamentary Procedure:

Personnel

Officer

Each person or **officer** in a meeting employing Parliamentary Procedure has a specific role and associated responsibilities. Ideally, you will be familiar with the roles of everyone present and abide by the rules of procedure. The very real stresses and pressures of heated discussion and debate, however, often test the membership's discipline and familiarity with the procedure.

Chairperson

The **Chair** can either be appointed or elected. If the Chair oversees a business concern, such as a board of directors, he or she is usually appointed. The Chair of a service meeting, such as the Lions Club, is usually elected for a specific term by the membership.

Regardless of the type of meeting being presided over, the Chair's responsibilities remain consistent. These are:

1.   to consult with the Secretary when drawing up the agenda.

2.   to remain impartial at all times.

3.   to call the members to order.

4.   to maintain order by granting permission to speak.

5.   to listen well and speak sparingly.

6.   to expedite proceedings.

7.   to facilitate, not obstruct, free speech.

8.   to periodically review important points in the discussion.

9.   to limit discussions of opinion when facts are available.

10.   to stimulate discussion.

11.   to end discussion and put the motion to vote.

12.   to break a tie vote (usually by voting against the motion).

13.   to countersign all reports and correspondence at the meeting's conclusion.

14.   to adjourn the meeting.

The Chair is the member best versed in the rules governing Parliamentary Procedure. Should he or she be unfamiliar with the rules, credibility and control of the meeting is quickly lost.

The Chair can best maintain order in a meeting by insisting that the membership address the Chair, thereby significantly reducing the number of out-of-order remarks. It is also the Chair's responsibility to champion the rights of individual members by disallowing tactless remarks and insisting on a restatement of emotional or frivolous statements.

If the Chair finds it impossible to maintain impartiality during the discussion of and vote on an issue, he or she requests another member to assume the Chair, takes the floor to make a statement, votes, and only then reassumes the position of Chair.

Secretary

The Secretary, or Recording Officer, also has an extensive knowledge of the rules of Parliamentary Procedure, as well as an intimate knowledge of past proceedings and prior submissions. As the organization's archivist or historian, the Secretary's knowledge is indispensable to the Chair's conduct of the meeting. Positioned next to the Chair during the meeting, the Secretary should be able to quickly produce the various documents required by the Chair.

The Secretary's duties are as follows:

1.   to assist the Chair in the drawing up of the agenda.

2. to inform the Chair if a **quorum** is present.

3. to call the meeting to order in the Chair's absence and to preside until the temporary Chair is elected.

4. to read the record or **minutes** of the previous meeting.

5. to keep the minutes of the meeting.

6. to write the minutes in an impartial fashion, avoiding any criticism, favourable or otherwise.

7. to maintain a consistency of style when writing the minutes, especially those to be published.

8. to receive the correspondence and read it during the course of the meeting.

9. to read the current minutes at any point in the meeting at the Chair's request.

10. to assemble all signed reports and correspondence at the meeting's conclusion for the Chair's countersignature.

11. to act as custodian of all papers belonging to the organization.

Treasurer

The **Treasurer**, or Financial Officer, is responsible for the duties normally associated with a banker. The Treasurer is the custodian of any funds deposited in the organization's name and disburses funds upon order of the organization and the Secretary.

The Treasurer's duties are:

1. to present an annual Treasurer's Report, both orally and in writing, at a predetermined time each (fiscal) year.

2. to release funds to various committees and individuals upon order.

3. to secure a receipt whenever funds are released.

4. to report to the organization each time a disbursement is made.

5.   to periodically have the auditing committee review the books and vouchers.

Committees

An important component of Parliamentary Procedure, the **committee** is usually assembled with one specific purpose in mind, and in most instances is dissolved when its work is completed. Perhaps the greatest service the committee provides is that of time-saver--it does the preliminary work in preparation for the final deliberation by the membership. This legwork most often includes research, analysis and discussion of the research, voting, and construction of a report.

The committee is theoretically subject to all the rules of Parliamentary Procedure, but it usually conducts its business in a more informal atmosphere. As an appendage of the main assembly, it is ultimately accountable to that assembly.

Most organizations recognize three types of committees:

- The **committee of the whole** consists of the entire assembly and is formed when the assembly has to consider a matter it does not want to refer to committee, or when it wants the freedom associated with a committee in its treatment of a subject.

- The **standing committee** is appointed for a set time and is operative or ready to act whenever it is called upon to do so. The standing committee does most of its work whenever new information on its project becomes available.

- The **select committee** is a special task force formed to consider one important matter. Select members are either appointed by the Chair or nominated by members of the general assembly. Their task is of the highest priority and is given immediate attention.

Committees, like general membership meetings, can only operate when a quorum is present. Many **constitutions** set a quorum at two-thirds or more of the membership. This is often the case where the membership is small. Large memberships often establish a quorum as a simple majority (half of the total membership plus one). If a quorum is not present, the meeting must be adjourned. Standing, and especially select, committees are carefully appointed to reflect a balance of members of all parties. When members miss a meeting, this not only jeopardizes achievement of a quorum, but creates an imbalance during the debate and voting process.

Where either the standing or select committees' tasks require specialized investigation or deliberation, the committees may appoint a **subcommittee** comprising some of its members. The subcommittee reports to the standing or select committee that appointed it. It ceases to exist once its work is completed.

The committee of the whole and the select committee are automatically dissolved upon receipt of their reports by the general assembly. The standing committee remains in existence until the end of its appointed term.

The committee and the subcommittee should be considered as meetings in miniature. They are managed by a Chair and are recorded by the Secretary. The report created by the committee majority is the official report to be submitted. If the committee minority wishes to communicate its position to the general assembly, the committee Chair may permit the minority to submit either one collective report or a number of individual reports. Minority reports can only be adopted by the parent meeting as a substitution for the majority report.

Members at Large

Meeting participants who are "without portfolio"--that is, without specific duties--are known as **members at large**. Members at large are usually invited to attend special sessions, such as annual shareholders' meetings, and can join the discussion after gaining the Chair's recognition, but are usually discouraged from making or seconding motions. Their primary purpose is to exercise their right to vote on issues affecting the organization or corporation.

Documents

Every organization requires both documented regulations governing its operation and records for its reference. All original documents are kept by the organization's Secretary, but copies are freely available to the membership.

Constitution

The constitution is the founding document of the organization, containing the rules and regulations governing that organization. It is usually the product of a committee and may be amended before adoption by all members at a meeting. The constitution contains the following information:

1. name and purpose of the organization.

2. number of officers and their functions.

3.   number for a quorum (the minimum number of voting members required to conduct business).

4.   frequency of meetings.

5.   method of amending the constitution.

Constitutions, once adopted, are purposefully made difficult to amend. A constitution that can be easily amended carries little weight. It also makes the mandate of the organization vulnerable to change. As a rule, a constitutional amendment must be proposed at a quarterly meeting and cannot be considered until the next quarterly meeting. This allows the membership time to consider such a major proposal.

By-Laws

Generally, a **by-law** is a rule adopted by the membership used to effect or enforce the constitution. By-laws are of such importance that they cannot be altered in any one meeting. Most organizations keep a separate set of by-laws called **rules of order**. These special rules describe how a meeting is to be conducted (the order of business, method of nomination and election, and regulations regarding the membership).

Agenda

The agenda is the working document for a meeting and indicates the order of business for that meeting. The agenda is drawn up by the Secretary in consultation with the Chair. Agenda items are received up to four days before the scheduled meeting. Members should have at least two days to consult the agenda before meeting. While the agenda is, in essence, a blueprint for the meeting, it should not be so detailed as to constrain the natural course of the meeting. The following items are found on most agendas:

1.   Call to Order

2.   Minutes of Previous Meeting

3.   Confirmation of Minutes

4.   Reports of Committees

5.   Correspondence

6.   Treasurer's Report (usually annual)

7.   Unfinished Business

8.   New Business

9.   Nominations (usually annual)

10. Elections (usually annual)

11. Adjournment.

Minutes

If you are the Secretary, your primary function during a meeting is keeping the minutes or the record of the meeting. Don't attempt to write everything down or you may miss an important point. The experienced Secretary develops a sixth sense of what to include and what to omit. Because minutes are both written and read, they must be concise, accurate, and grammatically sound. Record them in a permanent record book with a wide margin for corrections.

The Chair may request that you read a portion of the minutes at any point in the meeting to clarify the proceedings. It is imperative, then, that you keep abreast of the discussion. Most organizations require both the Secretary and the Chair to sign the minutes at meeting's end. You'll also be called upon to read the minutes of the previous meeting immediately after the meeting has been called to order. This helps to remind the membership of what occurred at the last meeting and is especially important if meetings are held infrequently.

Include the following elements in the minutes:

1.   *Call to Order*   Record the organization's name, the time and place of the Call to Order, the Chair's name, and the number of members present (in order to establish a quorum).

2.   *Confirmation of Minutes*   The minutes of the previous meeting, after any corrections, are adopted as read; indicate the **mover** and the **seconder**.

3.   *Reports of Committees*   Committee reports are read by committee Chairs. Reports are invariably moved for discussion under **New Business**; record the mover and the seconder.

4. *Correspondence* Indicate letters received since the last meeting as either filed or referred to New Business.

5. *Treasurer's Report* Separate the two primary elements, **accounts** and **bills**; record the mover and the seconder of any motions regarding this report.

6. *Unfinished Business* Read any motions made during the last meeting on matters interrupted by adjournment *exactly* as they appear in the minutes; record the movers and the seconders.

7. *New Business* Indicate the names of all movers and seconders in the handling of the reports of committees, referred correspondence, agenda items, and new motions from the **floor**.

8. *Nominations* Record the names of the nominees, the positions they are nominated for, and the nominators and seconders.

9. **Elections** Indicate the candidates' names, the offices being contested, the type of vote (usually secret ballot), and the results.

10. **Adjournment** Indicate the time of adjournment and how the meeting is adjourned (moved and seconded and approved by a vote, or declared adjourned by the Chair).

Reports

Reports of committees should follow a consistent format determined by the membership. Committee reports are modified versions of the committee minutes and should include the time and place of the meeting, the members in attendance, the business discussed, and recommendations arising from the discussion. A typed copy of the report is signed and dated by the committee Chair. After the report is read to the membership, it is presented to the Secretary. The report and its recommendations are discussed during the New Business segment of the meeting.

Deliberation

Voting

The method of **voting** and the number of votes required for a motion to pass are clearly indicated in the constitution. As a rule, either a two-thirds or a majority vote is required. By-laws vary: sometimes a two-thirds vote is defined as two-thirds of the entire membership; sometimes it means two-thirds of the membership present at the meeting. A majority is usually determined after a quorum has been established (a majority vote is half the membership present plus one).

The rules concerning the vote required for many motions are firmly established in parliamentary process, and are indicated under secondary motions.

A motion generally is put to the vote when no further modification (amendment) is required or if debate is exhausted. Voting can be initiated either by the Chair or by any member calling the question. The Chair usually determines the type of vote used in each instance; some types lend themselves better to certain issues than others. The Chair, as impartial moderator, does not exercise the right to vote. However, if there is a tied vote, the Chair usually votes against the motion, with each motion considered unpopular until it has passed. Should the Chair feel strongly about an issue up for vote, he or she can vacate the Chair during the discussion, appoint another member to temporarily assume the post, and vote.

Voting can be administered in a number of ways:

1. *Voice Vote* Also known as the yeas and nays vote, this method of voting can be conducted in two ways. The Chair can put the question before the floor and ask the membership for the vote in general terms. All in support of the motion will say *yea* simultaneously; then all in opposition to it will say *nay*, again simultaneously. This, of course, does not give an accurate measurement of support and is therefore used at the Chair's discretion when little opposition to the motion is expected.

    The voice vote can also be exercised on an individual basis (the roll call vote). The Chair reads the **roll** of members present and each member responds affirmatively or negatively, or abstains. The Secretary tallies the results and the Chair announces the decision.

2. *Rising Vote* The Chair asks the membership in favour of the motion to rise, then those opposed to the motion to rise. Either the Chair or the Secretary counts the votes. The Chair then announces the decision.

3. *Show of Hands* Rather than asking the membership to rise, the Chair can simply ask for a show of hands. As always, the affirmative question is put first. The Chair asks those in favour of the motion to raise their right hands, then asks those opposed and finally those abstaining from

the vote to do the same. Either the Chair or the Secretary counts the votes prior to the Chair's announcement of the decision.

4. *Teller Vote* This type of vote is especially useful when the membership is an inordinately large one. The Chair appoints an affirmative teller and a negative teller, one from each side of the question. The members are then counted by one of the tellers as they file by the teller of their choice. After receiving the teller counts, the Chair announces the decision.

5. *Ballot Vote* This method of voting is the most formal and is usually reserved for instances outlined in the constitution or by-laws. Sometimes called the secret ballot, it affords members anonymity when a contentious or contested issue is up for vote. Ballot votes are commonly used when the membership elects its officials. Ballots are usually prepared in advance of the vote and are distributed to the membership. After they are marked, the ballots are collected and counted by the Chair and two appointed members. The Chair then announces the decision.

Primary Motions and Amendments

Debate is the essence of parliamentary deliberation, but there is a logical progression that leads up to a vote. Any and all discussion leading to a resolution is subject to **motions** (or questions) and **amendments**. If you make a proposal for action in a meeting, you are the mover and are making a motion. If you want to make a counterproposal to limit, clarify, or correct a motion, you are making an amendment.

Each motion and amendment is given equitable consideration during the debate and ensuing vote. They are governed by strict guidelines. You can only propose a motion after you've been given permission to speak from the Chair. Unless there is some support for your motion, it cannot be debated by the membership. Whoever offers support for your motion is the seconder.

All motions must proceed, in order, through the following steps:

1. *Move* The mover makes the motion to put on the floor (subject of consideration).

2. *Second* Any person on the floor can second the motion. This indicates the motion has some popularity and is probably worth pursuing. Once it has been seconded, the motion has received official consideration (or is in possession of the membership or the **house**). The motion can now

only be withdrawn with the permission of the mover and seconder. The membership can then vote it down.

3.   *State*   The Chair restates the motion to ensure that all present clearly understand its intent.

4.   *Debate*   Any discussion of the motion can only occur if the speaker first gains permission to speak from the Chair. Because they are probably most familiar with the issue and obviously support the motion, the mover and seconder will speak first. Speakers must follow the direction offered by the Chair to keep this segment orderly.

5.   *Amend*   (This step is optional.) Should the original motion require modification at any point during the debate, an amendment can be proposed. Because an amendment is a motion, it must be moved, seconded, and approved by a majority vote. An amendment should always support and never contradict the motion. The original meaning of the motion can usually be maintained by not changing the verb in the motion.

There are two types of **amendment**: first rank amendments modify the original motion; second rank amendments modify first rank amendments. There can only be one amendment of each rank on the floor at any given time. Second rank amendments must be dealt with before those of the first rank are disposed of. Note that amendments of the third rank cannot exist; in other words, there cannot be an amendment to an amendment to an amendment.

6.   *Call*   Once discussion is exhausted, any member from the floor can **call** the question. This is a vote on whether to vote on the motion. If either two-thirds of the membership or the majority (as determined in the constitution) feel a vote is appropriate, then the Chair will **put** the question.

7.   *Restate*   The Chair rereads the motion to ensure that the membership understands it and is aware of any amendments made to it.

8.   *Put*   The question is put to the membership for vote by the Chair. The vote is usually conducted by a show of hands; the Secretary records the number of votes for and against the motion, and the number of abstentions.

9.   *Declare*   After the Secretary has tabulated the votes and abstentions, the Chair announces the result of the vote.

Secondary Motions

A secondary motion always concerns either the main motion or the conduct of the meeting. Secondary motions are useful to the Chair and members alike in that they provide a vehicle for streamlining and policing the meeting.

Secondary Motions dealing with the Main Motion

Here's a brief look at ways secondary motions can affect the main motion and how they must be employed:

1. *Withdraw the Motion* This overrides the motion it refers to and automatically stops discussion of that motion. It does not require a seconder, can neither be discussed nor amended, and must be approved by a majority vote.

2. *Amend the Motion* The motion to amend has precedence over the primary motion. It requires a seconder, can be debated and amended (by a second rank amendment), and must be approved by a majority vote.

3. *Limit Discussion of the Motion* This is a method of ensuring the motion is properly disposed of. Limiting its discussion guards against the minority's extending an obviously unpopular debate. This motion must be seconded, cannot be debated, and is subject to amendments. A two-thirds vote is required for it to pass.

4. *Lay on the Table* A motion to lay on the table means that a primary motion is negatively perceived; it may be reconsidered at a future meeting. This motion requires a seconder, can neither be discussed nor amended, and requires a majority vote.

5. *Take off the Table* A motion to take off the table means a previously tabled motion can be revived for consideration under New Business. This motion can only be made when no other motion is pending. It must be seconded, and can neither be debated nor amended. It requires a majority vote to pass.

6. *Suspend the Rules* This motion temporarily changes the order of business. It prevails over any motion it relates to. It must be seconded but can neither be discussed nor amended. This motion requires a two-thirds vote to pass.

7. *Shelve the Motion* This serves to effectively kill the motion by postponing it indefinitely. Usually the membership prefers not to vote either way on it. It overrides the primary motion, must be seconded, and can be discussed. This motion cannot be amended and requires a majority vote to pass.

8. *Postpone Discussion* Similar to the above motion, this too serves to postpone discussion, but only temporarily. It is usually proposed when more time for discussion of the primary motion is required or if a member familiar with the issue is absent. It must be seconded, can be debated, and can be amended. It requires a majority vote.

9. *Refer to Committee* When sufficient information is unavailable for an informed vote, a motion is made to strike a committee to investigate the issue and report back at a future meeting. This motion requires a seconder, is open to discussion, can be amended, and requires a majority vote.

10. *Put the Question* When any member believes that discussion on a primary motion has been exhausted, he or she can move that a vote be taken on that motion. It must be seconded, can neither be discussed nor amended, and requires a two-thirds vote to pass.

Secondary Motions dealing with the Conduct of the Meeting

Here's a brief survey of ways secondary motions can affect the conduct of the meeting and how they must be employed:

1. *Point of Order* When parliamentary rules are violated, any member can move a point of order. Such a motion has precedence over the motion to which it refers. It does not require a seconder and can neither be debated nor amended. The Chair resolves this point without membership input, though the decision can be appealed.

2. *Point of Appeal* Also known as appeal of decision of Chair, this motion requires a seconder and can be discussed if the Chair's ruling is on a debatable motion. It cannot be amended. An appeal must be made immediately after the Chair's ruling on an issue. The Chair has the option of stating the reasons for his or her decision prior to discussion. A majority vote determines if the original decision will stand.

3. *Point of Privilege* This motion is concerned with objectionable conduct or matters of comfort (such as the level of noise) in a meeting. It does

not require a seconder, cannot be debated, and cannot be amended. The Chair resolves this point, but the decision can be appealed.

4.   *Recess* Any member can move that the membership recess before continuing with the meeting. A **recess** is usually called for prior to a lengthy ballot count or to temporarily adjourn a lengthy meeting. This motion must be seconded and can only be discussed if no other motion is on the floor. It can be amended and requires a majority vote.

5.   *Adjournment* This motion overrides all others (except for the motion to set the time for the next meeting). It must be seconded, can neither be discussed nor amended, and requires a majority vote to pass. The Chair can also declare an **adjournment**.

The Chair and Meeting Management

Obviously, the pivotal officer at a meeting employing the rules of Parliamentary Procedure is the Chair. The Chair must not only manage the agenda, but must also quickly and effectively rule on breaches of meeting conduct. Familiarity with the rules will ensure a productive and equitable session for all.

No one expects a novice Chair to manage meetings flawlessly. If you've just become a Chairperson, the following guidelines should help you manage your duties and responsibilities during a meeting:

1.   When calling the meeting to order, state, "The meeting will now come to order." Continue with the proceedings after the Secretary determines if a quorum is present.

2.   Announce "The Secretary will read the minutes of the previous meeting." After the minutes are read, ask the membership if the minutes require corrections or additions. If any changes are made, ask the Secretary to reread the altered portion(s). When all present are satisfied with the minutes, announce, "There being no [further] errors or omissions in the minutes, I declare them adopted as read," and sign the minutes.

3.   Call upon the Chairs of committees to present their reports. When doing so, follow the order established in the agenda. Reserve any discussion of these reports for the New Business portion of the meeting.

4. Ask the Secretary to read the correspondence. After each letter is read, either direct it to New Business (for discussion) or have it filed. Comply with any request to redirect a letter from the file to New Business.

5. When the Treasurer's Report is on the agenda (usually once a year), request that the Treasurer read the report. The Treasurer's Report must have two distinct segments: **accounts** and **bills** (often termed expenditures). After it has been read, ask, "Does anyone move the adoption of the Treasurer's Report?" Request a seconder for the motion.

6. If any motions made and seconded during the last meeting were not disposed of, they must be considered under **Unfinished Business.** Ask the Secretary to read the motion exactly as it appears in the previous meeting's minutes, then continue with the debate of the motion. Handle all outstanding motions in this way until the Unfinished Business has been properly disposed of.

7. When handling the New Business segment of the meeting, proceed through the business in the following order:

    (1) *Reports* The Chair of the committee responsible for the report will move that recommendations in the report be adopted. The seconder of the motion is usually a committee member. The report can be adopted as presented, amended, or referred back to the committee for further work.

    (2) *Correspondence* Any correspondence directed to New Business should be reread by the Secretary to remind the members of its content. Its acceptance must be moved and seconded.

    (3) *Motions (Agenda)* Motions received before the meeting and placed on the agenda are the next items handled. The Secretary reads the motion and, if seconded, it is debated.

    (4) *Motions (From the Floor)* State, "The meeting is now open for New Business from the floor." Any member wishing to speak must first gain permission to do so. Announce, "The Chair recognizes [the member's name]." If a motion is made and seconded, then state the motion clearly and allow debate to proceed.

8. Nominations and elections are usually handled annually. Any number of nominations for an office can be made. Once a person has been nominated and seconded for a position, restate that person's candidacy

to the assembly. After nominations close, oversee the vote and announce the result.

9.   If no member moves for an adjournment and the agenda has been properly disposed of, announce, "I declare this meeting adjourned." If no motion is made to set the time for the next meeting, announce the date and time, referring to the constitution, which determines the frequency of meetings.

GLOSSARY

accounts the portion of the Treasurer's Report that refers to regular payments made by the organization, such as rent and telephone service.

adjournment formal closure of a meeting. May be moved, seconded, and supported by a majority vote, or declared by the Chair.

adjudicator the judge of a speech or debate. The adjudicator can work alone or as one of a panel of judges. Evaluations are usually written on adjudication forms, which offer commentary on elements of speech delivery and content.

adrenalin a powerful hormone that, when released into the bloodstream, stimulates the heart into beating faster (tachycardia). Also referred to as epinephrin.

agenda the document drawn up by the Chair and Secretary, with input from the membership, outlining the order of business of a meeting.

amendment a proposed change in the wording of a statement under consideration. A first rank amendment deals with the original motion. A second rank amendment deals with the amendment.

anagram the formation of a new word or phrase using the letters from other words or phrases. Anagrams are often used as mnemonic devices.

analysis the examination and explanation of materials researched for a presentation. The second stage of research consolidation, performed after information has been synthesized.

articulation the forming and sounding of words; enunciation. Ideally, articulation is clear and crisp.

audience desensitization the gradual introduction of more listeners to an audience while the speaker delivers a presentation. This gradual increase in audience size helps the speaker better cope with speaking before larger groups.

bar graph a graph indicating differences in quantity or distance, which are charted by means of vertical or horizontal bars of varying length, plotted on a graph. While not as accurate as the line graph, the bar graph has a greater visual impact.

baseline stress the average stress level present in the body at a given time. Serves as the marker point for stress measurement in individuals.

bills the portion of the Treasurer's Report that refers to irregular payments made by the organization, such as a computer system purchase or a building repair.

biofeedback the technique of raising or lowering normally unconscious or involuntary physical responses in the body. Heartbeat, blood pressure, and body temperature can be controlled by concentrating upon these responses.

body language the posture, gesture, facial expression, and dress of a speaker that, when analyzed, provide secondary messages about that person's comfort and clues on how to interpret any accompanying verbal message. Also referred to as kinesics.

brainstorm the process of suggesting and evaluating ideas in a group situation. One person is appointed to take notes while others in the group suggest ways of dealing with an issue or a theme. The ideas are evaluated and edited at a later time.

brainstorming a problem-solving exercise requiring members of a small group or committee to suggest solutions. Only after the suggestions are exhausted does the group discuss and evaluate them.

brief the battle plan or strategy for a debate, jointly constructed by team members. The brief provides a detailed outline of the proposed approach to the constructive segment of the debate.

burden of proof the obligation to show, through research and analysis, that the current situation (or status quo) is unacceptable. It is the responsibility of the pro (or affirmative) side in a debate.

burden of rebuttal the duty to rebut the changes proposed by the affirmative side, through defending the status quo or criticizing the proposals as insufficient or worse than the current system. It is the responsibility of the con (or negative) side in a debate.

by-law a rule adopted by the membership to uphold the constitution.

cadence the consistent rise and fall or rhythmical modulation of an individual's voice.

call the vote posed to the membership on whether or not to vote on a motion.

capillaries extremely small blood vessels that connect the smallest veins to the smallest arteries.

Chair alternatively referred to as the Chairperson. In a formal meeting, the Chair is the elected or appointed presiding officer at a meeting employing the rules of Parliamentary Procedure.

cognitive having to do with perception, recognition, and understanding.

committee a group of members appointed to research and report on a subject of particular interest to the membership. A committee employs the rules of Parliamentary Procedure and is accountable to the parent assembly.

committee, of the whole a committee comprising the entire assembly. It is formed when the membership does not want to appoint a specialized committee or wants to operate under committee rules.

committee, select a special task force formed to consider a high priority matter.

committee, standing a committee appointed for a set time that is operative or ready to act when relevant information becomes available.

constitution an organization's founding document containing its mandate, rules, and regulations.

constructive speeches the speeches delivered during the first round of a debate. These speeches establish the team's position on the issue debated.

contour an unbroken line on a contour map joining points of like elevation or depression above or below sea level. Contour lines never intersect.

contour map a map indicating the topography of a portion of the earth's surface by means of contour lines. Contour maps show the steepness or grade of topographic slopes; contour lines that are close together indicate steep slopes.

critical stress the stress point at which an individual's performance begins to decline because of stress.

debate a formal argument between two opposing sides on a pro or con issue.

decoder(s) in interpersonal communication, the listener(s).

deductive a method of reasoning that moves from the general to the specific. In a speech, the discussion is initiated with generalizations and culminates with specific examples.

delivery (physical) the total impression communicated by a speaker's posture, movement, gesture, visual contact, and facial expression, usually in conjunction with a verbal message. Delivery is also referred to as body language.

delivery (vocal) the total impression communicated by a speaker's projection, pitch, articulation, pronunciation, and timing, usually in conjunction with a physical message.

descriptive speech one of the four varieties of informative speech. It offers a clear and detailed description of a person, place, or thing.

encoder in interpersonal communication, the speaker.

explanatory speech one of the four varieties of informative speech. It offers a detailed explanation of a process or event and includes background information, clarification, and periodic summaries.

exploded the separation of component parts in a graphic or diagram, used to better indicate the relative positions of those parts to each other and to provide a better view of a specific component.

fight or flight the instinctive assessment of danger, resulting in two options--fighting the danger or fear, or fleeing it. Speakers who experience this syndrome either struggle slowly through their presentations (fight), or quickly proceed through them (flight).

fine gestures understated gestures that provide subtle secondary messages to an audience. Fine gestures are primarily performed with the hands and fingers.

floor the forum granted by the Chair where a member is the recognized speaker.

flow chart a chart indicating the sequential flow of a process or the relationship between components of a system.

forum the question and answer period, open to the audience, in a symposium.

gross gestures obvious, often dramatic, gestures that serve to illustrate major points of a presentation. They are usually performed with the arms and upper part of the body.

house the membership assembled at a meeting.

hyperactivity excessive activity or restlessness associated with physical or emotional discomfort.

hyperventilation excessive and often erratic breathing, frequently associated with fear or stress.

inductive a method of reasoning that moves from the specific to the general. In a speech, the discussion is initiated with specific examples and culminates in a general statement.

inflection the variations in tone or pitch of the voice. Inflections serve to endow the verbal message with secondary instructions. They are often a cultural trait.

information overload the reception of an overwhelming amount of information in a brief time, resulting in reduced comprehension and retention.

instructional speech one of the four varieties of informative speech. This type of speech relies upon the logical ordering and simple presentation of the steps of a procedure. It is also referred to as the process speech.

intonation the manner of sounding words through changes in stress and pitch, which can alter the melody and thus, the meaning of a verbal message.

isobar an unbroken line on a barometric map joining points of like barometric pressure. Isobars chart pressure increases and decreases, indicating probable weather changes. Isobars never intersect.

isometric exercises physical exercises involving equal but opposing stresses and pressures. Isometrics place muscles in opposition to each other (i.e., at chest level, the palms of the hands pushing against each other).

isotherm an unbroken line on a temperature map joining points of like temperature. Isotherms never intersect.

jargon the specialized language of a group or profession that, because of its exclusivity, is difficult for non-members of that group or profession to understand.

judge either the Moderator or a member of the judging panel of a debate. The judge decides the winning team in a debate.

key a portion of a map, diagram, or chart devoted to the explanation of symbols used in the graphic.

kinesics any body movements that can b analyzed to provide deeper insight into a person's verbal or nonverbal message. Kinesics are also referred to as body language.

line graph a graph incorporating the vertical and horizontal axes and plotting a trend. The vertical or y-axis usually indicates units; the horizontal or x-axis usually indicates time.

meeting a formal gathering of a membership for the discussion and/or resolution of particular issues.

members at large members of the broader assembly who join the membership (usually once a year), primarily to voice their concerns and to vote.

minutes the written record of a meeting kept by the Secretary.

mnemonic devices schemes or strategies developed to enhance memory. Anagrams are common mnemonic devices.

Moderator the person who presides over a symposium, panel, or debate.

motion, main the proposal for action made by the mover. This motion usually requires a seconder to achieve consideration by the house.

motion, secondary a motion that deals with either the main motion or the conduct of a meeting.

mover the member who proposes a main or secondary motion.

New Business the portion of a meeting devoted to the adoption of reports, the discussion of correspondence, and the handling of motions.

officer any member of the house with a specific title and function.

organization chart a chart indicating a hierarchy of officers or organizational structure. The head of the organization is always found at the top of the chart; officers with the least responsibility and power are found at the bottom of the chart.

overlay a multiple transparency used with an overhead projector. Each transparency layer contributes to the audience's greater understanding of the visual. Often each overlay will employ different colours to enhance viewer comprehension.

panel a small group presentation, instructional in nature, delivered by experts in a given topic.

panning the process of moving the eyes slowly and steadily across a subject or audience.

paralanguage the language that is expressed beyond the obvious or overt message. Paralanguage comprises two major components: paralinguistics and kinesics.

paralinguistics the vocal component of paralanguage. Paralinguistics is the study of how the verbal message is delivered, focusing especially on inflection and intonation. It is also referred to as voice.

parameters limiting or defining features or rules governing the scope of a presentation.

parliamentary presentation a formal meeting conducted before an audience that incorporates the rules of Parliamentary Procedure, derived from the British parliamentary system.

Parliamentary Procedure set of rules governing the conduct of a meeting derived from the British parliamentary system.

physical map a map indicating the physical features of a specific geographic area, including elevations, depressions, and bodies of water.

pictograph a graph using symbols or pictures to represent real numbers or proportions. A symbol is representative of a number of units, indicated in the key. Comparisons can be made by showing symbols of objects compared in proportionate sizes. Pictographs using symbols as representative units indicate the numeric value of the symbol in the key.

pie graph a graph indicating percentages as slices of a pie. The larger the slice, the greater the percentage of the whole it represents.

pitch the frequency (highness or lowness) of sound produced by a speaker. Ideally, pitch is modulated to influence the audience.

political map a map showing political borders and boundaries. This type of map usually indicates cities, towns, villages, and seats of government.

presentational speech one of the four varieties of informative speech. It is an account of collected data and other research-related information with the aim of illustrating the course and relationship between the elements of that process.

prewriting the preparation stage of speech construction. Prewriting incorporates the research performed by the speaker and results in a skeletal outline.

primary research information generated by the speaker's own surveys and experiences. This type of information cannot be found in libraries or other traditional information sources.

projection the force or "carrying ability" of a speaker's voice.

proposition, in a debate the statement upon which the debate is based. It is always worded as a resolution.

proposition, in a persuasive speech the assertion or statement made by the speaker. The speaker attempts to prove the proposition using supporting evidence and persuasive techniques.

proxemics the study of personal, interpersonal, and group space as it relates to communication. It includes analysis of the space people keep between themselves and objects during communication.

put the term used when a motion or question is presented to the membership by the Chair for vote.

quorum as defined by the constitution, the minimum number of members required to be present for an official meeting.

rebuttal the counter-argument, presenting evidence in opposition to the other team's evidence in a formal debate.

rebuttal speeches the speeches delivered during the final round of a debate. These speeches contradict the evidence presented by the opposition during the constructive segment of the debate.

recess a temporary adjournment of a meeting during a ballot count, or an agreed upon break during a lengthy meeting.

relief map a map indicating the topographical features of a specific geographic area by means of colour or shading. Increasing elevations are shown by increasingly darker shades of brown; decreasing depressions are shown by increasingly darker shades of green.

resolution the proposition for debate, worded to encourage both fairness and argument between two debating teams.

rhetorical question a question posed for effect and not expecting an answer.

Robert's Rules of Order the nineteenth-century American manual of meeting procedure, based on the rules of Parliamentary Procedure.

roll the list of members present at a meeting.

rules of order a special set of by-laws describing the conduct of a meeting.

schematic chart a chart showing the functional relationship between mechanical, electrical, or electronic components.

second the member of a debating team, usually not the leader, who speaks second in both the constructive and rebuttal rounds of a debate.

secondary research information which has already been compiled (in print or on tape) by persons other than the researcher. Secondary research is traditionally found in libraries. Books provide the bulk of the information; magazines, newspapers, and journals provide the most current printed information.

seconder the member who officially supports a main or secondary motion by seconding it after it is moved.

Secretary alternatively referred to as the recording officer, the organization archivist in charge of keeping all documents. The Secretary helps the Chair construct the agenda, often counts votes, and keeps the minutes of the meeting.

stammering the very visible, often painful, effort to sound words. Stammering is characterized by repetitions and hesitations and is usually embarrassing to the speaker.

state anxiety the anxiety instigated by one particular stressor. This anxiety is progressive until the stressor is removed.

status quo the current system or situation, defended by the con (or negative) side in a debate.

strategy a comprehensive presentation plan which anticipates the direction of the presentation and offers a loosely structured plan for action.

stressor an object, event, or task that causes stress in an individual.

stuttering the repetition of a sound in an effort to speak. This habit usually involves the jerky repetition of initial consonants when forming a word.

subcommittee an appointed arm of a standing or select committee that under-takes specialized research and reports back to its parent committee.

summary chart a chart showing comparisons or outlining a process. It is used to provide a lot of information in a few words.

sympathetic nervous system the nerves of the nervous system which control some involuntary functions of the body.

symposium a series of relatively brief presentations on a common topic, theme, or issue.

syntax the way in which words are arranged and used in a language.

synthesis the collection and organization of research from various sources to suggest general patterns or trends.

systematic desensitization the therapy that teaches anxiety-prone individuals to relax certain muscle groups. During the visualization stage of the process, the person imagines a stressful situation and systematically desen-sitizes those muscles in order reduce tension.

tactics reactive changes in strategy used either to maintain a stated position or to counter an opposing argument.

territorial used to describe a tendency toward possessiveness about a specific place, space, or object. A person who insists upon sitting in the same seat in a classroom can be described as territorial.

thesis statement a concise, one-sentence statement that encapsulates the spirit and intent of an oral or written presentation. It is also referred to as the topic sentence.

trachea the tube extending down from the larynx (which contains the vocal cords) to the bronchi (the two main branches entering the lungs). It is also referred to as the windpipe.

trait anxiety anxiety believed to be acquired genetically. This form of anxiety is characterized by constant and pervading stress, not brought on by any particular stressor.

transcription the first of four steps in the prewriting process. Transcription involves the listing of information collected during research and the ideas generated by this research.

transitional device in speaking, any aural or visual prompt provided to help the audience move from one idea to the next.

Treasurer alternatively referred to as the financial officer. The Treasurer serves as the organization's banker; he or she disburses funds, keeps records, and presents an annual financial report.

Unfinished Business the portion of a meeting devoted to the discussion and handling of motions made during the previous meeting.

vertigo the severe dizziness or giddiness that often accompanies disorientation.

visual aid an adjunct, such as an object, picture, model, chart, or diagram, used in an oral presentation to enhance audience understanding of the speech content.

visualization the act of visualizing or imagining a stressful event. It is a stage of systematic desensitization therapy.

vocal cords the cords of membrane found in the larynx or voice box. When air released from the lungs passes between the vocal cords, they vibrate, producing sound.

voice the vocal component of paralanguage, which focuses on the verbal delivery of the message. Voice is also referred to as paralinguistics.

voting the process of accepting or rejecting a motion, requiring either a two-thirds or majority vote from the membership.

working model a fully or partially operating model of a mechanical object, often constructed to scale.

x-axis the horizontal axis of a graph. It usually indicates time as the variable in a line graph.

y-axis the vertical axis of a graph. Units are indicated on the vertical axis of a line graph.

SOURCES

Baird, John E. *Speaking for Results*. New York: Harper & Row, 1981.

Barnard, Sandie. *Speaking our Minds: A Guide to Public Speaking for Canadians*. Scarborough, ON: Prentice-Hall Canada, 1990.

Bormann, Ernest G., and Nancy C. Bormann. *Speech Communication: A Basic Approach*, 3rd ed. New York: Harper & Row, 1981.

Crampton, Esme. *Good Words, Well Spoken: A Handbook of Speech*. Toronto: The Norman Press, 1980.

DeVito, Joseph A. *The Elements of Public Speaking*. New York: Harper & Row, 1981.

Dunckel, Jacqueline, and Elizabeth Parnham. *The Business Guide to Effective Speaking*. Vancouver: Self-Counsel Press, 1984.

Eisenson, Jon, and Paul H. Boase. *Basic Speech*, 3rd ed. New York: Macmillan, 1975.

Eisenberg, Abne M., and Teri Kwal Gamble. *Painless Public Speaking*. New York: Macmillan, 1982.

Fausti, Remo P., and Edward L. McGlone. *Understanding Oral Communication*. Menlo Park, CA: Cummings, 1972.

Forde, Thomas H. *The Principles and Practice of Oral Dynamics*. New York: Exposition Press, 1964.

Gregory, Hamilton. *Public Speaking for College and Career*, 2nd ed. New York: McGraw-Hill, 1990.

Gruner, Charles R. *Plain Public Speaking*. New York: Macmillan, 1983.

Howell, William S., and Ernest G. Bormann. *The Process of Presentational Speaking*, 2nd ed. New York: Harper & Row, 1988.

Kelly, Louis G. *25 Centuries of Language Teaching*. Rowley, MA: Newbury House, 1976.

Lucas, Stephen E. *The Art of Public Speaking*, 3rd ed. New York: Random House, 1989.

McCabe, Bernard P., and Coleman C. Bender. *Speaking Is a Practical Matter*, 4th ed. Toronto: Allyn and Bacon, 1981.

Metcalfe, Sheldon. *Building a Speech*. Toronto: Holt, Rinehart and Winston, 1991.

Monroe, Alan H., and Douglas Ehninger. *Principles of Speech Communication*, 7th brief ed. Glenview, IL: Scott, Foresman, 1975.

Nelson, Paul Edward, and Judy Cornelia Pearson. *Confidence in Public Speaking*, 2nd ed. Dubuque, IA: Wm. C. Brown, 1984.

Potter, Simeon. *Our Language*. Harmondsworth: Penguin, 1957.

Riggs, D.A. *A Guide to Public Speaking*. Guelph, ON: University of Guelph, 1978.

Robert, Henry M. *Robert's Rules of Order*. Toronto: Coles, 1989.

Samovar, Larry A., and Jack Mills. *Oral Communication: Message & Response*, 7th ed. Dubuque, IA: Wm. C. Brown, 1989.

Stuart, Christina. *Effective Speaking*. London: Pan, 1988.

Tiffany, William R., and James Carrell. *Phonetics: Theory and Application*, 2nd ed. Toronto: McGraw-Hill, 1977.

Vasile, Albert J., and Harold K. Mintz. *Speak with Confidence: A Practical Guide*, 4th ed. Toronto: Little, Brown, 1986.

Verderber, Rudolph F. *The Challenge of Effective Speaking*, 6th ed. Belmont, CA: Wadsworth, 1982.

Walter, Otis M., and Robert L. Scott. *Thinking and Speaking*, 5th ed. New York: Macmillan, 1984.

Whitman, Richard F., and Paul H. Boase. *Speech Communication: Principles and Contexts*. New York: Macmillan, 1983.

Zelko, Harold P., and Frank E.X. Dance. *Business and Professional Speech Communication*, 2nd ed. Toronto: Holt, Rinehart and Winston, 1978.

To the owner of this book:

We are interested in your reaction to *Speaking for Success: The Canadian Guide* by Anthony Lieb.

1. What was your reason for using this book?

_____ university course _____ continuing education course
_____ college   _____ personal interest
                           _____ other (specify)

2. In which school are you enrolled? _____

3. Approximately how much of the book did you use?
_____ 1/4 _____ 1/2 _____ 3/4 _____ all

4. What is the best aspect of the book?

5. Have you any suggestions for improvement?

6. Is there anything that should be added?

fold here

(fold here and tape shut)

0116870399-M8Z4X6-BR01

Heather McWhinney
Publisher, College Division
HARCOURT BRACE & COMPANY, CANADA
55 HORNER AVENUE
TORONTO, ONTARIO
M8Z 9Z9